Legacy of
The Revolution

THE VALENTINE—VARIAN HOUSE

Lloyd Ultan

THE BRONX COUNTY HISTORICAL SOCIETY
Bronx, New York

Copyright © 1983 by The Bronx County Historical Society. All rights reserved under International and Pan-American Copyright Conventions. Published in the United States of America.

Cover by Alan J. Pellegrini
Book design by Alvin Schultzberg

Library of Congress Cataloging in Publication Data
Ultan, Lloyd.
  Legacy of the Revolution.

  Bibliography: p.
  Includes index.
  1. Valentine-Varian House (New York, N.Y.)
2. Valentine, Isaac—Homes and haunts—New York (N.Y.)
3. Varian, Michael, 1808-1893—Homes and haunts—New York (N.Y.) 4. Bronx (New York, N.Y.)—Dwellings. 5. New York (N.Y.)—Dwellings. 6. Vernacular architecture—New York (N.Y.) 7. New York (N.Y.)—History—Revolution, 1775-1783. 8. Bronx (New York, N.Y.)—History. I. Title.
F128.68.B8U585   1983   974.7'1   83-7384
ISBN 0-941980-12-X

THE BRONX COUNTY HISTORICAL SOCIETY
3309 Bainbridge Avenue, The Bronx, New York 10467

Gary D. Hermalyn, Editor

This volume is dedicated in gratitude
to the memory of

WILLIAM CHARLES BELLER
and
THEODORE KAZIMIROFF

who separately and together labored
to preserve the Valentine—Varian
House for future generations

ABOUT THE AUTHOR

Lloyd Ultan is an Associate Professor of History at the Edward Williams College of Fairleigh Dickinson University in Hackensack, New Jersey, and had served as President of The Bronx County Historical Society from 1971 to 1976. He is the author of the highly acclaimed *The Beautiful Bronx (1920–1950)* and is an editor of *The Bronx County Historical Society Journal*.

ACKNOWLEDGMENTS

This work was written with aid and grants from the National Endowment for the Humanities to write a history of The Bronx, which enabled me to uncover much of the source material. Support also was received from the New York City Department of Cultural Affairs, and from the Hon. Stanley Simon, President of the Borough of The Bronx. I am also grateful for the co-operation and encouragement of my colleagues at Edward Williams College of Fairleigh Dickinson University, who agreed to provide me with the time to get the job done. I wish to thank the staff at the New York Public Library, the New-York Historical Society, the Huguenot Historical Society and the Bronx Office of the City Register for their aid and co-operation. I also wish to thank Ples Felix, Jr., Jay Filan, Anthony King, John D. Mitchell, Alice Richardson, Stephen Stertz and Saul Weber who helped uncover the material. The staff of The Bronx County Historical Society is to be especially commended for their enthusiastic co-operation, and above all, Gary Hermalyn, the Executive Director, whose energy and drive helped make this possible. Of course, all views and interpretations of the facts are my responsibility alone.

PREFACE

No one has previously written a study in depth of the incidents surrounding the Valentine-Varian House. Therefore, some myths have grown up about the structure. Neighborhood residents fondly believe that George Washington must have slept in the old stone house, although there is no evidence to support this claim. At the time of its relocation to its present site, the *New York Times* variously cited the date of its construction as 1770 and 1775, neither of which is correct.

It is certain that the house is an old one. It has been named a landmark of New York City, and is on the National Register of Historic Places. While the aspect of the house is pleasing, there are no real extraordinary architectural details which would have set it aside from other structures of the period. Similarly, its history does not record ownership by nationally significant persons, nor does it provide the site for a nationally important event. Yet, it is this very lack of national significance which makes the Valentine-Varian House important. It is a rather typical house of the period, illustrating better than many more outstanding architectural monuments how ordinary people lived. Moreover, the house was involved with aspects of a national event—the American Revolution—which are usually overlooked in textbooks, but which had a profound effect on the lives of the people of the time. The Valentine-Varian House had a central role in these aspects which affected the surrounding neighborhood, and this is the story of the interaction between the house and the neighborhood during that event.

Sources written at the time the incidents occurred, or memoirs of those who took part in them, have been relied upon almost exclusively. The histories of The Bronx were used only for those events which happened within the authors' memories.

TABLE OF CONTENTS

One .... THE OLD STONE HOUSE ON
　　　　　　 BAINBRIDGE AVENUE 1

Two ...... 1758–1773: YEARS OF PROLOGUE 3

Three ..... 1774–1776: YEARS OF PREPARATION .. 11

Four ...... 1777: YEAR OF BATTLE 27

Five ...... 1778–1783: YEARS OF PERIL 41

Six .... 1784–1792: YEARS OF RECOVERY 59

Seven ..... SINCE 1793: YEARS OF
　　　　　　 PRESERVATION 69

Appendix .. THE ARCHITECTURE OF THE
　　　　　　 VALENTINE-VARIAN HOUSE 100

　　　　　　 NOTES 107

　　　　　　 BIBLIOGRAPHY 118

　　　　　　 INDEX 123

LIST OF ILLUSTRATIONS

Map. The Bronx during the American Revolution,
    from Otto Hufeland's *History of Westchester
    County During the American Revolution*,
    published in 1926 5

Map. Historical Sketch Map of Kings Bridge by
    Thomas Henry Edsall, from J. Thomas Scharf's
    History of Westchester County, Volume I,
    published in 1886 8

Richard Montgomery, Isaac Valentine's neighbor 10

George Clinton, whose troops occupied Isaac Valentine's
    farm in October, 1776 21

William Heath, whose troops occupied the Valentine
    House in January, 1777 28

Robert Rogers used the Valentine House as a
    headquarters in February, 1777 33

Israel Putnam commanded American troops in an
    engagement involving Isaac Valentine's house
    In November, 1777 39

The Comte de Rochambeau, commander of the French
    forces in America, may have slept in the Valentine
    House in July, 1781 55

Richard Morris, Chief Justice of New York State,
    who restored order in the area of the Valentine
    House following the withdrawal of British troops
    in May, 1783 57

Isaac Leggett Varian, Mayor of New York, 1839–1841 79

The Valentine-Varian House in 1874 or 1875. Oldest
    known photograph of the structure 81

The Valentine-Varian House in 1899 83

The Valentine-Varian House in 1905 85

The Valentine-Varian House soon after the west wing
    had been destroyed 86

The Valentine-Varian House in April, 1934 87

The Valentine-Varian House in 1956 89

William Charles Beller about 1961 92

The Valentine-Varian House in 1963 94

The side and rear of the Valentine-Varian House in 1963 95

Moving the Valentine-Varian House across Bainbridge
    Avenue in 1965 96

Dr. Theodore Kazimiroff in 1966 97

The Valentine-Varian House, Memorial Day, 1966 98

Students from St. Pius High School examining
    exhibits in the Valentine-Varian House, May, 1976 99

The last remaining original door in the Valentine-
    Varian House 103

West section of the attic of the Valentine-Varian House
    in 1971 104

The restored Valentine-Varian House on its new site
    in 1975 106

CHAPTER ONE

The Old Stone House on Bainbridge Avenue

On the east side of Bainbridge Avenue at East 208th Street in New York City's Borough of The Bronx stands an old stone house. Two stories high with an attic, it is set in a landscaped lot of about three-quarters of an acre (three-tenths of a hectare), facing westward across a bustling urban street. It is located in a neighborhood of apartment houses, one- and two-family dwellings, and local shops. Behind it rises a small slope bearing grass, shrubs, and trees that marks the boundary of the neighborhood park where the elderly may rest and the young may play such vigorous games as basketball, baseball, and tennis.

An occasional passerby may stop to notice the quaint architecture of the old stone structure. He may also notice a sign identifying it as the Valentine-Varian House. Why, he may wonder, is it still standing in this neighborhood when so many such houses in similar circumstances have been destroyed through the years? There is no sign there to tell him. If he should question after whom it is named, or what happened in the house that could lead to its preservation in modern times, no visible marker can inform him.

Indeed, a passerby admiring the old stone house on Bainbridge Avenue would never realize that it was not built on its current site, but moved there from its original location less than 100 yards (about 91 meters) away. In fact, it was once situated at the northwest corner of Bainbridge Avenue and Van Cortlandt Avenue East, and, at that time, faced southward. Nor could the passerby realize that the old stone house played a role in the events that led to the establishment of the nation.

The story of this house is long and complicated. In fact, it begins in the middle of the eighteenth century.

CHAPTER TWO

1758–1773: Years of Prologue

By the mid-eighteenth century, the Dutch Reformed Church in New York City was in serious financial trouble. For almost three-quarters of a century, it had owned a huge tract of land south of Spuyten Duyvil Creek extending from the Harlem to the Bronx Rivers in what was then Westchester County. It was called the Manor of Fordham, and by terms of the will bequeathing it to the church, the institution was to use the income from the manor to pay the salary of its ministers. Nevertheless, by the mid-point of the century, the amount of cash raised by renting farms to sturdy families, mostly of Dutch ancestry, was lower than the cost of administering the land itself. Plagued by constant court suits contesting its control of the property, and by a noticeable decline in available timber resources, the Church had to sell the land and re-invest the proceeds in other real estate to support its ministers.

Therefore, the Dutch Reformed Church obtained a legal ruling enabling it finally to divide the manor into lots for sale. A notice was tacked up on the doors of St. Peter's Church in the township of Westchester, just east of the Bronx River, announcing the sale of the property.

While the Dutch Church owned Fordham, the manor had remained separate from any local municipality, although, by virtue of its patent, the town of Westchester claimed the territory. Once the Church completed its sale of the property, the entire Manor of Fordham would come under the jurisdiction of that town.

Word of the availability of the land spread quickly, and one of those who showed interest was a young blacksmith from

Yonkers named Isaac Valentine. At first, he seems to have been interested in the farm occupied by Frederick Bruin, but so was John Vermillye, Jr., who eventually obtained it. Undeterred, Valentine was willing to purchase the neighboring property. For the sum of £934 to be paid in four yearly installments by May 1st, Valentine received a farm, a wood lot and a piece of swamp ground by signing a deed of lease and release on January 30th and 31st, 1758. When he placed his signature on the documents, the blacksmith gave the representatives of the Dutch Reformed Church four bonds secured by a mortgage.[1]

Isaac Valentine's new farm was well situated. It was located on gentle slopes separated by a small valley through which flowed a modest creek. Today, this small valley is the course of Mosholu Parkway. The eastern boundary of his property was the Bronx River, and the western end was near the precipitous cliff that dropped down toward Spuyten Duyvil Creek. (Today, the western boundary would be somewhat west of Jerome Avenue.)

Through the property ran the curving road which led travelers from Boston to New York over a bridge at the Bronx River to the King's Bridge over Spuyten Duyvil Creek. Already in use for more than eighty years, it was the route used by riders carrying the mail between the two great cities linked by the thoroughfare. For that reason, it was called the Boston Post Road. (Today, Van Cortlandt Avenue East is a remnant of that highway.) However, the post riders were hardly the only ones using the road. Farmers frequently drove their cattle to market in New York City on Manhattan Island, raising dust clouds as the bovines trod the dirt path. Travelers on horses, in carriages, or on foot often passed by. Carts filled with milk and dairy products, lumber, fruit, wheat, and flour carved ruts in the road with their wheels.[2]

It was only natural that Isaac Valentine should build his home by the side of the road in the middle of his property. Not only would this give him access to the news that travelers would bring, and place him near to the major transportation artery in the area, but it would be good for his business. For a blacksmith in the midst of a rural area, the Post Road would

1748–1773: YEARS OF PROLOGUE

provide an easy means for customers to come to him for nails, shovels, rakes, hoes, and metal parts for harnesses, ox yokes, and other implements for the farm, and for pots, utensils, candlesticks, or other household items. In addition, if a cart or carriage should break down along the road, a nearby black-

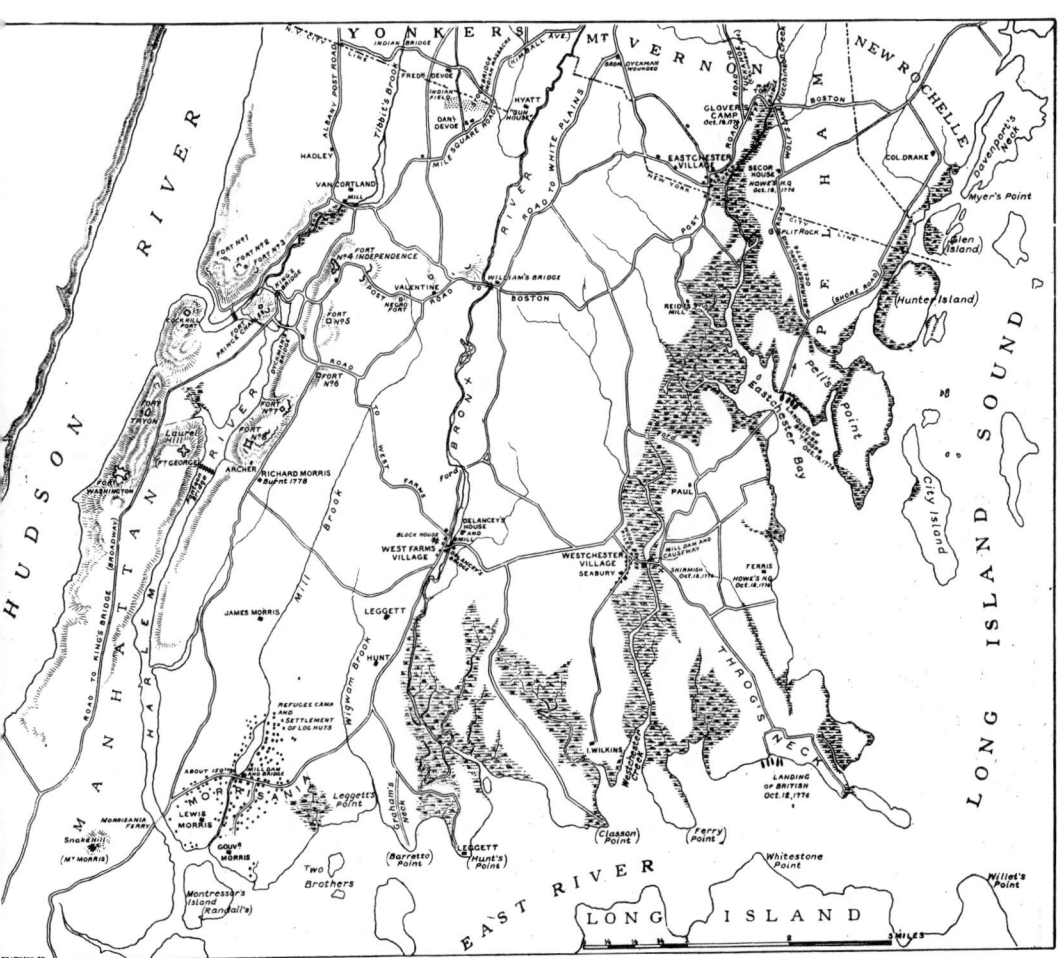

The Bronx during the American Revolution from Otto Hufeland's *History of Westchester County During the American Revolution*, published in 1926. Isaac Valentine's house is situated on the Post Road to Boston. *The Bronx County Historical Society Collection.*

smith would be certain to get the job of making the necessary repairs.

There, by the side of the road, Isaac Valentine built his farmhouse, using stones found in the field for the exterior walls and wood lined with chestnut laths for the interior. Wide boards were hewn from pine trees on the property to make the floors. All the carpentry work inside was held together by the nails the blacksmith made from his own forge. (Much of the work survives today and can still be seen in the house.)

As his needs grew, the blacksmith enlarged his dwelling over the years. Most likely, his first house was a simple one-story room with a pitched roof. Later, to the east of the first edifice, he built a larger two-story house with an attic, connecting it to the first by a small passageway. The larger structure was made with a central hallway having four rooms on each floor. Two fireplaces heated the two largest rooms on each story and the cellar. Since Valentine was a blacksmith, not an architect, the structure probably looked like the typical stone farmhouses of the era in the vicinity. Indeed, the nearby Van Cortlandts, who had completed their home about ten years prior to Valentine's purchase, lived in a home with similar features.

Near the house, Valentine constructed what everyone then called out buildings. These included structures to shelter his livestock, store his crops, and hold his blacksmith's forge.

Like other farmers in the neighborhood, Isaac Valentine divided his large farmland into separate fields. The same ground that had provided the stone for the exterior walls of his house also provided the material for the stone fences that separated the pasture from the orchard, the cultivated land from the woodland.

It was to the farm and his new house that Isaac Valentine brought his wife, and it was in this house that their three sons and two daughters were born. It was here that he prospered and grew to be one of the wealthiest men in Westchester County, easily ranked among the top 20% to 25% of the county's inhabitants in terms of the value of his landed property in 1768.[3] By the laws of the day, this entitled him to vote for members of the colonial legislature, to serve on juries, and to run for office. However, Isaac Valentine never was nominated for public office, and thus never served in one.

While it may be true that he was not interested in such service, Isaac Valentine would not be silent when he believed that his interests were at stake. His house was located about two miles (just over three kilometers) along the highway from the King's Bridge, the only land connection he and his neighbors had with Manhattan and New York City at the southern end of the island. The bridge was owned by Frederick Philipse, one of the wealthiest landowners in the colony. By law, Philipse charged the farmers for every cart and every farm animal which crossed it. Since the city was the major market for the farmers' products, the burden of these tolls was onerous.

It was for this reason that Benjamin Palmer and John Vermillye of Westchester County joined with Vermillye's brother-in-law, Jacob Dyckman of Manhattan, in 1758 to build the Farmer's Free Bridge, which was opened to the public in January, 1759. This had the effect of eliminating tolls on the King's Bridge as well. The cost of this improvement was borne solely by the builders, who had hoped to be reimbursed by the colonial assembly. However, Frederick Philipse was a member of the assembly, and in a powerful position to prevent the legislature from passing any act to relieve the distress of those who had ruined a lucrative enterprise of his own.[4] The bill to relieve the bridge's builders was quashed, despite the fact that the petition to the assembly urging compensation of £700 for the three builders was signed by about 190 prominent citizens from both New York and Westchester Counties. Among the 69 petitioners from Westchester County was Isaac Valentine.[5]

Although this act showed where Valentine's political sympathies lay, such expressions were rare, and he spent most of his time attending to his blacksmith's forge, his family, and his farm. In fact, the work of attending to both the blacksmith's business and the farmland was so large that he obtained a small number of slaves to aid him. Slavery was then legal, and it was not unusual for a family in the area to own a slave or two to help with the housework, with milking the cows and reaping the harvest, or with making the constant small repairs needed on the house and out buildings.

At times, business matters caused Isaac Valentine to be

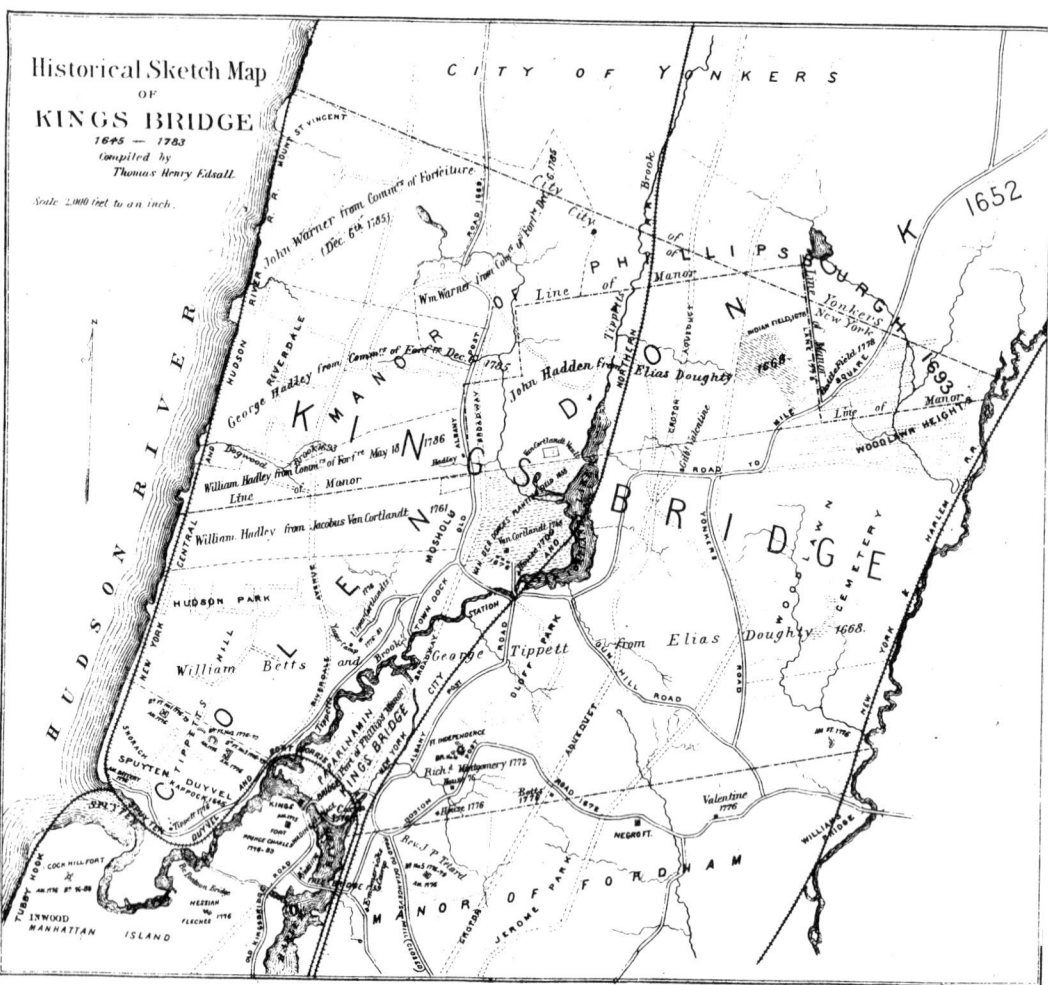

Historical Sketch Map of Kings Bridge compiled by Thomas Henry Edsall from J. Thomas Scharf's *History of Westchester County*, volume I, published in 1886. The Valentine House is located in the northern section of the Manor of Fordham. *The Bronx County Historical Society Collection.*

called elsewhere, and his stone house by the side of the busy Boston Post Road would be empty for the moment. It was deserted at such a time on Wednesday, July 7, 1773, when a stout, round-shouldered, dark-complexioned passerby, wearing a faded snuff colored coat and striped trousers, broke into the building to rob it. He got away with a deep blue broadcloth coat lined with white durant and having gilt buttons, a deep blue jacket, a pair of black knit breeches lined with white linen with the pockets patched with coarse pale blue cloth, and a fringed black handkerchief. In making his getaway, the thief was spotted heading westward toward the King's Bridge, and it was supposed he was headed for Philadelphia. Isaac Valentine offered 40 shillings reward for the capture of the villain, but it is not known whether he recovered his lost clothing.[6]

By the 1770s, the immediate neighborhood of the Valentine farm had changed only slightly. In March, 1772, John Vermillye, who owned the farm just to the west, advertised its sale.[7] The purchaser, Valentine's new neighbor, was a distinguished one—Richard Montgomery, an Irishman who had risen to the rank of lieutenant in the British army, and who was the brother of the Countess of Ranelagh. However, Montgomery, on July 23, 1773, married the daughter of the eminent colonial judge, Robert R. Livingston, and had decided to live in Rhinebeck in Dutchess County. He placed his Westchester County farm up for sale, but for years, no one wished to purchase it, and it remained in his possession.[8] Immediately to the south of Montgomery's farm, John Peter Tetard, a minister of the French Protestant Church in New York for 15 years, opened a French boarding school at his house, advertising for students in August, 1772. He taught his pupils French and such sciences as geography, the doctrine of the spheres, ancient and modern history, and logic. For those who wished preparation to attend a college or university, he offered instruction in Latin and Greek and reading in the classics.[9]

Travel along the bustling Boston Post Road was increasing. In June, 1772, Jonathan and Nicholas Brown announced the start of an experimental stagecoach service between New

York and Boston via Hartford, a round trip that would last for two weeks. Two coaches each left Boston and New York at the same time, meeting at Hartford before continuing the journey.[10] The coaches and their passengers had to pass by Isaac Valentine's stone house.

Despite the progress, the bucolic rural neighborhood in which Isaac Valentine built his house would soon be beset by controversy and violence. In fact, a war that would engulf much of the North American continent and involve several of the major powers of Europe would be brought right to the doorstep of Isaac Valentine's house.

Richard Montgomery, Isaac Valentine's neighbor. *The Bronx County Historical Society Collection.*

CHAPTER THREE

1774–1776
Years of Preparation

The dispute between the American colonists and the government of Great Britain probably seemed remote to Isaac Valentine, his neighbors and the farmers of the town of Westchester at the start of 1774. Nevertheless, the coercive measures of mid-1774, passed by the British Parliament to punish Boston for the deliberate dumping of tea into the harbor, were too high handed for many Americans. A Continental Congress was called at Philadelphia to deal with the situation.

With all the traffic on the bustling Boston Post Road, Isaac Valentine probably never noticed a stocky Boston silversmith galloping by the fieldstone farmhouse in early October, 1774. This was Paul Revere, who arrived at New York City on October 4th on his way to Philadelphia with messages to deliver to the Congress.[11]

By April, 1775, the tension between Great Britain and her colonies had exploded into military action at Lexington and Concord in Massachusetts, and a second Continental Congress at Philadelphia now had to handle these new circumstances. On May 25th, this Congress took note of the strategic nature of the King's Bridge as the only land connection between New York City and the mainland. It was imperative that communication between the city and the country not be severed, and the Congress resolved to take and fortify a post at King's Bridge for that purpose.[12]

However, some delegates to the New York Provincial Congress thought that building a fortification at King's Bridge was not necessary. After all, the fighting was in the Boston area, and New York City was not in danger of attack from the mainland. Moreover, building a fort costs money, and in light of the military situation as it then existed, the expense did not appear to be justified.[13] No fort was built at that time.

Therefore, nothing particularly untoward disturbed the life of Isaac Valentine and his neighbors throughout the spring of 1775. The war seemed remote, and the fighting was in a distant place. However, in June, Paul Revere once again galloped by the Valentine farmhouse, passing through New York City on June 25th on his way to Philadelphia with dispatches for the Continental Congress.[14] This time, too, he probably was hardly noticed.

However, it would have been difficult to overlook a traveler headed in the opposite direction on June 27th—an exceptionally tall Virginian in military uniform accompanied by a light horse troop from Philadelphia. This was George Washington on his way to assume command of the American army besieging the British in Boston.[15] It would not be the last time he would pass by Isaac Valentine's house.

During the summer of 1775, Isaac Valentine first felt the effects of the war. In May, in the same resolution that called for the fortification of King's Bridge, the Continental Congress had resolved that the militia of New York be armed and trained to act at a moment's warning. By August, the Westchester County committee had divided the county into militia districts, with the entire town of Westchester constituting a single district. This included areas referred to as the Manor of Fordham and West Farms, both west of the Bronx River, and the center of the town east of the river near today's Westchester Square. The committee members from the town called the inhabitants together at the town center on August 24th to form a militia company and to choose officers.[16] Isaac Valentine went, accompanied by his eldest son, Isaac, Jr., who was then two months short of his eighteenth birthday, and they were duly enrolled in the militia company. Nicholas Berrien was the only man from Fordham chosen to be an officer, the company's first lieutenant.[17]

Perhaps they felt slighted, or, more likely, they felt the inconvenience of the long distances those living west of the

Bronx River had to travel to the town center for training. In any case, the company members from Fordham and West Farms petitioned the New York Congress to make their area a separate district. They pointed out that, while it was believed there were not enough men on their side of the river to fill a separate militia company, in fact there were more than 70 men there able to bear arms, and that they had always been considered a distinct district previously. They asked that the inhabitants of Fordham and West Farms be able to form their own company and elect their own officers. The petition was signed by 81 men headed by Fordham's only elected officer, Nicholas Berrien. Isaac Valentine, the wealthiest landowner in the area, signed second, while his son, probably because of his youth, signed tenth.[18]

The petition was received by the New York Committee of Safety on September 5, 1775, and referred to the Westchester County committee which had drawn the boundaries for the militia districts in the first place. On September 11th, the county committee noted that no one from Fordham or West Farms had appeared to support the allegations in the petition, so a subcommittee was appointed to investigate the matter. The plea of the petitioners was granted when the county committee determined that Fordham and West Farms should be a separate militia district, and the triumphant militia members gathered on October 21st to elect their new officers. Nicholas Berrien was chosen their captain, but Isaac Valentine was not elected to any of the remaining positions.[19] This is not surprising considering Valentine's general reluctance to take a leadership role.

If organizing the militia brought the effects of war to Isaac Valentine, evidence of the war itself was brought directly to his farm and his stone house by the fall of 1775. On August 24th, the cannon were removed from the Battery in New York City to prevent them from falling into the hands of the British. Under the direction of Abraham P. Lott, they were moved to the area of the King's Bridge,[20] and were strewn in a line on the slope of a hill beginning about 250 to 500 yards (about 225 to 450 meters) north of Isaac Valentine's stone house toward the house of John Williams on the other side of Williams's Bridge across the Bronx River.[21]

Four months later, on Wednesday evening, January 17, 1776, a party of five men led by William Lownsberry of Mamaroneck set out from New Rochelle at 10 o'clock dressed in great-coats and hats. Their faces covered with handkerchiefs for protection against the piercing cold and howling wind, they traveled southward toward Williams's Bridge. In a bag, they carried a number of spikes fashioned by blacksmith Isaac Gidney, assisted by fellow blacksmith Joseph Purdy, from files purchased in New York City and from steel bars furnished by Lownsberry. They also carried two stolen sledgehammers. These Tories, Americans who supported the British side in the war, were determined to render the guns useless by driving the spikes into the touchholes of each cannon where the gunpowder would normally be ignited to fire the piece. Methodical as they were in doing the deed, there were far too many cannon in the fields for them to spike them all, and they had to leave without completing their job.

That night, the only person who heard anything untoward was Peter Valentine, the blacksmith's second oldest son, who was able to hear the ring of metal as the spikes were being driven into the cannon, first in one batch and then another. Isaac Valentine did not hear of the incident until his neighbor, John Williams, invited the blacksmith to cross the bridge to the east bank of the Bronx River to see the spiked cannon in the Williams's field. Valentine accepted the invitation, and looked with wonder at the sight. Isaac Valentine, Jr., did not discover that the cannon were spiked until a drover driving cattle before him from New England to New York on the Boston Post Road mentioned it to the blacksmith's son. The youth immediately informed his father's journeyman, an Englishman named William Dickin. Peter Valentine first told his father about hearing the cannon being spiked four days after the incident.

As soon as the New York Committee of Safety discovered that a large number of cannon were spiked, an independent battalion from New York City was dispatched to Valentine's and Williams's farms to guard the guns from further harm.

However, that guard was needed for city duty, and the committee called upon Lieutenant Colonel Lewis Graham to relieve the troops with Westchester County minutemen.

The New York Committee of Safety immediately began investigating the affair, questioning closely all who were involved and incarcerating everyone implicated. In telling their tale, those who committed the crime admitted spiking only the cannon at Williams's Bridge, but not those near Isaac Valentine's house. Several told of observing another party that same night dressed in dark clothes spiking cannon near the blacksmith's residence. Moreover, one stated that he had observed a light at one or two o'clock in the morning emanating from a window in Valentine's old house, which now served as a kitchen, and where Valentine's journeyman, William Dickin, slept. This was most probably the west wing of the house which the blacksmith had built before constructing the two-story dwelling to which it was attached.

With this testimony, suspicion quickly fell upon Isaac Valentine, who, after all, was a blacksmith, and the committee ordered Jonathan Blake, commander of the cannon guard, to send down to New York City Isaac Valentine, his journeyman, and all men in his family, keeping them apart so that they could not talk to each other. On January 30, 1776, the blacksmith, his eldest son, and his journeyman, under a guard of seven men, were delivered to the Committee of Safety and examined. It was clear that these men took no part in the affair. While Isaac Valentine knew William Lownsberry, he had not seen him nor any other member of the party that spiked the cannon that night, and did not know who did the deed. His son did not even know William Lownsberry. The youth admitted he was home the night the cannon were spiked, but had no knowledge of any light that was lit in the house. The English journeyman, William Dickin, denied he had a light lit at one or two o'clock in the morning, and saw no persons in the household who came in late. Undoubtedly, Isaac Valentine was readily believed because of his wealth, which gave him standing in the community, and because of his service in the militia.

However, if those who were guilty of spiking the cannon in John Williams's fields refused to admit the same in Isaac Valentine's, and if the blacksmith did not do it either, who had done it? The New York Committee of Safety began a futile search for the culprits. In March, 1776, Cornelius McCartney of Yonkers was accused of committing the act. He was a schoolteacher who had quarrelled with his students over a raffle, and, out of spite, his students accused him of spiking the cannon at Valentine's. It was obvious that the hapless scholar was not to blame, since he was teaching night school at the time, and he was discharged. The last person actively suspected of doing the deed was Joshua Ferris, the son of Caleb Ferris. Joshua Ferris was captured on August 8, 1776, but when he was examined, New York City was in military peril, and he was questioned on other matters, not the cannon. Seven decades after the event, Augustus Cregier related the tale that the deed was done by John Cocks, the tavernkeeper at the King's Bridge, and John Corbie of New York.[22]

Meanwhile, the cannon had to be guarded against further destruction, and those damaged had to be repaired. Isaac Valentine undoubtedly believed he could profit from the situation. A guard composed of one captain, one lieutenant, two sergeants, one corporal, and fourteen privates looked after the cannon. These men had to be fed, and arrangements were made for Valentine to provide board for six of the privates for ten shillings a week. Thus, for the time being at least, the stone house served as a temporary tavern.[23]

Nevertheless, the cost of such a large outlay worried officials in the New York Congress. If the cannon were concentrated on the Valentine farm, rather than spread out onto the Williams farm as well, fewer men would be needed to guard them. By March, 1776, John Williams was willing to move the fifty guns on his property for two shillings apiece, and David Barclay offered to guard them all at Valentine's farm with only six men. A committee recommended that seven men guard the cannon once they were all collected on Isaac Valentine's property and that David Barclay do it for £13 per week, exactly half the usual weekly outlay. The New York Congress adopted the recommendation enthusiastically.

While the cannon were being guarded, the spikes were being removed from their touchholes by heating each gun. This softened the metal spikes prior to drilling them out. Of course, two or three cords of wood were needed for each fire. Undoubtedly, these were hewn from timber standing on Valentine's property and, no doubt, the blacksmith charged the army for the use of his trees. As a blacksmith, it is also likely that Valentine's services were utilized in the process. By March, 1776, 82 of the cannon were unspiked this way and more were being worked upon.[24]

On June 10, 1776, the first shipment of cannon was removed from its resting place on the slope north of Isaac Valentine's stone house, and the process was repeated again on June 23rd. At that time, they were needed to protect New York City. However, some cannon remained on that hill until August of 1776,[25] a total of eleven months since they had been deposited there. By then, people of the neighborhood were calling the site cannon hill or gun hill. (Today's Gun Hill Road from Jerome Avenue to the Bronx River roughly parallels the site where the cannon were originally placed.)

By that time, the center of military action had shifted from Boston to New York, where the American army under Washington and the British army under General Sir William Howe, stared at each other across the wide expanse of Upper New York Bay. Suddenly, the area near the King's Bridge assumed the military importance envisioned when the Continental Congress first resolved to fortify it. Shortly after the troops began to remove the cannon from Isaac Valentine's farm, George Washington personally viewed the grounds above the King's Bridge and noted seven strategic places where fortifications could be built. He immediately ordered that the works be constructed, and directed two Pennsylvania battalions to begin them, intending to add other units as time went on. The Pennsylvanians arrived on June 21st.[26]

On July 5th, the day after the Continental Congress adopted the Declaration of Independence, General Thomas Mifflin assumed command of the American troops at King's Bridge. He immediately saw the possibility of the British attacking the heights above the bridge as a diversion, and noted that the fortifications there were not in good order. In response, increasing numbers of troops were assigned to this post throughout July and August with orders to complete the works. On August 8th, the New York State Convention appointed General George Clinton to command all state troops raised in Ulster, Orange, Dutchess, and Westchester Counties and ordered him to march to the fort already erected north of the bridge. Two days later, the Americans began to erect another fort on a hill overlooking the King's Bridge on the farm that Richard Montgomery could not sell and within sight of Isaac Valentine's stone house. (Montgomery, who had become a general in the Continental Army, had led an expedition to Quebec, where he had lost his life. His neighbor, John Peter Tetard, had gone with him as interpreter and had not returned, remaining an army chaplain. Thus, neither were in the vicinity when the King's Bridge forts were being built.) On August 12th, both Mifflin's and Clinton's brigades were placed under the command of Major General William Heath, who was to give the orders there as long as the American army held that ground. Four days later, Clinton was ordered by the State Convention to build carriages to remove the cannon from Isaac Valentine's fields for use in the King's Bridge fortifications. By August 23rd, the new fort on Montgomery's land was completed and dubbed Fort Independence. Troops were deployed around it, with Colonel Thomas Thomas's regiment camped just to its south with orders to occupy it if an alarm should be given. The following day, provisions were made for mounting the cannon in place, and by September 10th, those in Fort Independence were ready to be used as a warning signal in case the King's Bridge were attacked.[27]

Throughout this period, it is unlikely that Isaac Valentine was idle. In addition to attending to his farm throughout the summer, it is probable that his blacksmith's forge was used for profit in forming metal parts for the carriages carrying the cannon away. No doubt he also provided the wood for a fee. It is also likely that the business of providing food and drink for some of the soldiers continued as well, for General Heath referred to Valentine's house as a tavern as late as October.[28]

By that time, the American military situation had become worse. Washington's troops were hastily evacuated from Long Island because of Howe's advancing armies in August, and, in September, they had retreated up Manhattan Island to evade British flanking movements. The American commander was headquartered at Harlem Heights, giving Fort Independence and the King's Bridge fortifications enhanced importance. In this situation, Washington was willing to call out the local militia only as a last resort to defend its home territory in case the British should land on the east bank of the Harlem River.[29] He did not have a high opinion of the abilities and loyalties of Isaac Valentine and his fellow militiamen. In fact, he was more concerned that their livestock—the cattle, horses, hogs, and sheep which were needed by the army—be secured by driving them to the interior part of the county away from the war zone.[30]

On October 3, 1776, preparations had to be made in case the British attacked the mainland. Colonal Thomas Thomas's 2,258-man regiment occupied Fort Independence and the lines east of the fort. A troop of 158 light horse under the command of Major Backus of Connecticut also occupied the Boston Post Road between Valentine's stone house and Williams's Bridge. If the British attacked anywhere west of the Bronx River, ten light horse were to gallop to Major General Heath to serve as express riders. If the attack came east of that river, those men were to go to the front and to send express riders to the general to keep him informed. In the meantime, Heath knew more fortifications would be needed to repel any such assault, and, at a council of brigadier generals, he ordered additional works to be built, including a redoubt above Williams's Bridge.[31] (The site of that today is roughly the southeastern corner of Woodlawn Cemetery.)

On October 12, 1776, the British made their move, landing a large force on Throg's Neck. To defend King's Bridge and the American army in northern Manhattan from an attack from the eastward, two or three brigades marched along the Boston Post Road on October 14th, passing Isaac Valentine's house, to take up positions to the east of Williams's Bridge. On

October 17th, General Heath posted two regiments in Fort Independence and one to the east of it. Another regiment was placed in the redoubt overlooking Williams's Bridge, which Heath called the redoubt at Cannon Hill. Out of General George Clinton's New York State troops, Colonel Levi Pawling's regiment was stationed in Isaac Valentine's corn field, and Colonel Morris Graham's regiment was posted just north of it.[32]

Throughout this great alarm, it appears that Isaac Valentine's militia company was not called upon to assist. It is to be remembered that Washington did not trust the local militia and wished it to be used to defend its home ground only as a last resort. Nevertheless, that time soon arrived.

On October 18th, General Howe made another maneuver, transferring his army from Throg's Neck to Pell's Point, today in Pelham Bay Park. To mask his intentions, he organized a diversionary attack on the American works in the center of the town of Westchester (near today's Westchester Square). General Heath, observing the diversion near the spot, sent an express rider galloping to the commander of the brigade at Isaac Valentine's stone house ordering him to organize his men for a march to the scene of the diversion. Heath himself arrived at the house just as the brigade had completed its preparations, and the general ordered the officer to tell his troops to march, and he accompanied them on their journey. Near his objective, Heath was met by Washington, who ordered him to return the brigade to its previous location to prepare for a possible attack on the King's Bridge from the direction of Morrisania. Heath immediately obeyed.[33]

The next day, General Heath called Isaac Valentine's militia company into service for the only time recorded throughout the American Revolution. Referring to it as the Home Guard, Heath needed it to fill the gaps in his stretched-out forces, and the company was assigned no specific duties. Despite their knowledge of the neighborhood, other troops were assigned regular night patrols, with the rounds made once an hour. The outer limits of these patrols included the road in back of the woods north of Isaac Valentine's woods.[34]

In any event, Valentine's military career would prove to be short-lived.

The decision had already been made that the American army's position at King's Bridge had been made vulnerable, and the troops were ordered to march northward to White Plains. The evacuation began on October 20th, but, on the

George Clinton, whose troops occupied Isaac Valentine's farm in October, 1776. Portrait by Ezra Ames, 1795. *Courtesy of The New-York Historical Society.*

following day, Colonel John Lasher was ordered to remain at the King's Bridge post with 600 men until further orders.[35] By the night of October 23rd, the evacuation of all but the 600 was completed.[36]

It was probably at this time that Isaac Valentine's militia regiment dissolved. Certainly, desertions among the regular troops ordered to remain at King's Bridge were high. By October 26th, only 400 out of the original 600 men remained at their post, each averaging only ten rounds of ammunition a man. Colonel Lasher, to his horror, found only six artillerymen left at Fort Independence, and only thirty rounds of ammunition remaining there. Moreover, the fort was in bad order. The situation was growing desperate, with the enemy occupying Mile Square in Yonkers and spotted on Spuyten Duyvil Hill. Lasher pleaded with Heath, who was at White Plains, for orders.[37]

Heath ordered Lasher to remove the cannon and stores at Fort Independence to Fort Washington on Manhattan, which continued to be occupied by American troops. He was to burn his barracks and dash for White Plains via Dobbs Ferry, but if the road were blocked, he was to go to Fort Washington. Relieved, Lasher quickly executed his orders.[38]

However, a large army of Hessians, troops hired in Hesse, Germany, to fight for the British, under the command of Lieutenant General Freiherr Wilhelm von Knyphausen, had marched from New Rochelle to Yonkers, and with six battalions at his disposal, the Hessian commander was able to frustrate Lasher. Although the barracks were duly burned, the Hessians, following a skirmish with the Americans, were able to occupy King's Bridge. Captain John Montressor, leading 300 Hessians and three men of the 17th Light Dragoons, succeeded in capturing 12 four-pounder cannon at Fort Independence, while the defenders fled for safety to Fort Washington.[39]

While these events were taking place, Isaac Valentine and his neighbors faced an unpleasant choice. They could follow the American army northward, seeking ground that would place their families safely out of the war zone while the men continued to fight. However, this would leave their property unprotected, open for any military use, and ripe for plunder, which would result in financial ruin. Moreover, if the property were abandoned, it was likely that each family would be forced to live as refugees, surviving on the charity of others. For Isaac Valentine, who was one of the wealthiest men in the county, this choice was unpalatable.

The other alternative was to remain on the property under British and Hessian occupation, trying to live a normal life under trying circumstances, while giving as little aid and comfort to the enemy as possible. While such an alternative was filled with greater personal risk than the first, at least it afforded the opportunity to minimize any possible destruction of property and to restrain any plundering. This is the choice that Isaac Valentine and most of his neighbors took.

This decision was probably prompted by the actions of several American soldiers when they had occupied the area from August through October of 1776. As early as August 18th, General Heath heard complaints that field and gardens were being pillaged, a practice which he condemned as a disgrace and for which he threatened severe punishment. On September 8th, he had to remind the troops that pulling down and burning fences and pillaging corn fields were strictly forbidden, and on September 29th, he had his officers take care that houses and other buildings were not injured.[40] While there is no evidence that Isaac Valentine's property was plundered, it is certain that those of some of his neighbors were.

In addition, Washington's desire to secure the livestock from the area by driving the animals to safety to the center of the county prompted the New York Committee of Safety on October 14th to order all horses, hogs, sheep, and cattle driven away from the area exposed to the enemy, with the farmers paid compensation. The Westchester County farmers were also ordered to thresh their grain so that the army could use the straw, but Washington was also empowered to seize unthreshed grain for a price. If that were not enough, the threshed grain itself could be seized by the chairman or deputy chairman of the county committee, also providing compensation for the farmer. The Americans, in their zeal to carry out their

LEGACY OF THE REVOLUTION

orders, at times forgot that farmers needed to retain enough livestock and seed to begin work the following year, and, in effect, the seizures seemed no different than pure plunder. Washington, recognizing this, ordered that enough be left to the farmers of the area so that they could increase their livestock and begin planting in the future.[41] Undoubtedly, Isaac Valentine was affected by these orders.

It was with this in mind that Isaac Valentine stayed on his farm, living in his stone house. He may have been wise, for on the very day that General Knyphausen took possession of Fort Independence, a British officer noted that his troops, and the Hessians in particular, were unmercifully pillaging the countryside, thus producing a reaction against the British cause among the farmers. Of most concern to Isaac Valentine, on November 4th, the Waldeck regiment, German mercenary troops usually lumped with the Hessians in the American mind, occupied the redoubt near his house overlooking William's Bridge.[42]

Knyphausen's men stayed in the neighborhood, joined by the main British army under General Howe, who established his headquarters in the Van Cortlandt house on November 13th and at DeLancey's Mills near West Farms the following day. Howe remained there until after the Hessians captured Fort Washington. Major General James Lee Grant, the commander of the 3rd Battalion of Light Infantry, was quartered at John Williams's house, near where the 23rd regiment was encamped and near a post occupied by a picket of the 16th dragoons. Since the Waldeck regiment was aiding in the capture of Fort Washington, it is likely that the latter two positions were the redoubt overlooking Williams's Bridge and Isaac Valentine's house respectively. On November 15th, the men at each of the three positions were joined by a corporal and six dragoons.[43]

While the British occupied their positions throughout November, they used the opportunity to repair the fortifications in the vicinity left by the Americans. It is likely that, on this occasion, the troops threw up a small earthen fortification on a hill on the Valentine farm overlooking the Boston Post

Road near Isaac Valentine's stone house. (It later came to be called Negro Fort, so-called from a black detachment in British pay being headquartered there, and was near where Van Cortlandt Avenue East and the Grand Concourse cross today, atop the hill at St. George's Crescent.)[44]

Once Fort Washington was captured, Howe's design was to spend the winter in New York City while sending Lieutenant General Earl Cornwallis into New Jersey to chase Washington. Accordingly, on November 17th, he ordered some of Knyphausen's Hessian brigades under Major General Martin Conrad Schmidt to Fort Washington and to take command of Fort Independence and Spuyten Duyvil. General Grant's 3rd Battalion of Light Infantry at Williams's house was replaced by the 1st and 2nd Battalions. On November 19th, the latter two units, along with several others, were placed under the overall command of Lord Cornwallis and were ordered to prepare to move. At 9 o'clock in the evening, these soldiers crossed Williams's Bridge, passing by Isaac Valentine's stone house, to get to the Hudson River to cross into New Jersey. The 23rd regiment still occupied the redoubt overlooking Williams's Bridge. Below their high position, on the Boston Road, on Isaac Valentine's farm, the British stored their hay supply. On November 22nd, each regiment sent a quartermaster, twelve men and a wagon to receive its share of the hay and orders from Quartermaster General Sir William Erskine, and by the 23rd, the army had moved to New York City.[45]

Left behind were sufficient troops to defend the King's Bridge fortifications. Under the overall command of General Knyphausen, a 24-hour guard consisting of a captain and sixty men was established in Fort Independence. Of greater importance to Isaac Valentine, Colonel Robert Rogers's Rangers were posted on his farm, with a detachment of a captain and sixty men assigned to the redoubt overlooking Williams's Bridge.[46]

An American native, Colonel Rogers had achieved some fame in the French and Indian War by raising a unit which had fought effectively in the west. A Tory in the current contest, he had raised a similar regiment to serve the British, calling it the Queen's American Rangers, recruiting his men from fellow Tories. Disdaining the standard British red uniform, Rogers insisted that his troops wear green as a more suitable color for backwoods combat. Zealous and irascible, he had already earned the enmity of many Westchester County farmers by driving off their livestock for army use. He was to do so again. By November 25, 1776, his Rangers had collected 1,200 sheep, 900 hogs and several hundred cattle in the town of Westchester, driving them to Willett's Point (today's Clason Point) for shipment to New York.[47] Since the American army the previous month had left barely enough to restock the herds, many farmers faced ruin. In light of the fact that the Rangers were quartered on Isaac Valentine's farm, it is unlikely that the blacksmith's livestock escaped their notice.

The plight of these citizens certainly did not escape the notice of the New York State Convention, the body then acting as the state's legislature while a constitution was being written. Its members wanted to do something especially to protect them and their property and also to secure the effects of those who had fled behind American lines or who had joined the American army. On December 19th, the Convention resolved to mount a secret expedition into the area using Dutchess and Westchester County militia units, possibly aided by Continental troops.[48]

Unfortunately, the secrecy of the expedition was not maintained, and, within a week, even the Hessians learned about it. To meet the expected attack, a Hessian brigade was sent to reinforce the King's Bridge area,[49] and it was probably at this time that a small detachment occupied Isaac Valentine's house.

Nevertheless, General William Heath recommended to Washington that the raid still be executed as a diversion which might ease the pressure on the American army in New Jersey.[50] Thus, the stage was set for Isaac Valentine's stone house, which had stood on the periphery of a war zone, to become the center of battle.

CHAPTER FOUR

1777: Year of Battle

As the new year dawned, George Washington began to look favorably upon General Heath's recommendation for a diversionary attack at King's Bridge. He ordered Heath to move down to New York with a considerable force of about 4,000 militiamen from New England. The assault was to appear as if it were the first stage of an attack upon the city to force the British to withdraw a large number of their troops facing the main American army in New Jersey to meet the supposed threat. Heath had also suggested that he use this opportunity to collect all the forage he could find in the vicinity to keep it out of the enemy's hands that winter, a prospect of which Washington also approved.[51]

On January 13, 1777, Heath began moving his army southward in three columns. Two days later, a deserter from the enemy lines at King's Bridge was interrogated, giving the general valuable information as to the number and disposition of the troops in the area. On the evening of January 17th, the three columns began moving to the vicinity of their target. The westernmost column followed the Albany Post Road paralleling the Hudson River. The easternmost column, commanded by Brigadier General David Wooster, came down the Boston Post Road from New Rochelle and arrived at Williams's Bridge just before sunrise on January 18th. Meanwhile, the center column, led by Brigadier General John Scott with Heath accompanying, set off from White Plains down the Mile Square Road (of which Van Cortlandt Park East north of Woodlawn Cemetery is a remnant today), halting on the hill behind Isaac Valentine's stone house.[52]

William Heath, whose troops occupied the Valentine House in the siege of Fort Independence in January, 1777. *Courtesy of The New-York Historical Society.*

From the deserter, Heath knew that a number of guards was quartered in the farmhouse, but he did not know if the guards would defend it if he attacked. Therefore, he ordered Captain Lieutenant David Bryant, who commanded the few artillery pieces on the expedition, to bring a field cannon to the advance guard to cannonade the house if there were any opposition from it. In case the guards decided to flee to the safety of Fort Independence, Heath ordered 250 men to move westward and then double back by pushing into the small valley between the house and the fort (today's Mosholu Parkway). Before this maneuver could be completed, the sun had risen above the eastern horizon, and two of the enemy's light horsemen on reconnaissance duty came over the hill on the Boston Post Road as it descended toward Williams's Bridge, coming face to face with the head of General Wooster's easternmost column. The two riders attempted to turn around, but before they could do so, the Americans fired a cannon at them, causing one to fall off his horse and be captured. The other galloped toward Fort Independence, passing Isaac Valentine's house and Negro Fort, yelling, "The Rebels! The Rebels!"

Thoroughly alarmed, all the outguards and pickets posted in Valentine's fields started to run toward Fort Independence for safety, some leaving their arms, blankets, tools, and provisions behind. The guards who fled from Isaac Valentine's house and from Negro Fort were fired upon as they ran, but none were killed. The Americans ran after them in hot pursuit, and were able to capture one hapless defender who was not as fleet as the rest.

Heath immediately ordered detachments to occupy both Negro Fort and Isaac Valentine's house. In the house, a search by the Americans uncovered ten muskets that the fleeing guards had left behind. For Isaac Valentine, who lived there, the experience must have been bewildering. Within a handful of minutes at dawn of January 18, 1777, his house and farm changed from being an outpost for the British side to a base for the American cause. In the process, his house had become a military target, and his farm, a battlefield.

With the hill, the house and Negro Fort secure, the remainder of General Wooster's men poured across Williams's Bridge and the rest of General Scott's militiamen came down the hill behind the stone farmhouse to occupy the small valley between the house and Fort Independence. Heath then sent a summons to the Hessian commander at the fort, offering generous surrender terms. However, the garrison, manned by Hessians and

Roger's Queen's Rangers, returned a verbal refusal of surrender. With that, the siege of Fort Independence began. It was to last eleven days, until January 29th.

On the morning of January 19th, the day after the siege began, the enemy drew first blood. As an American detachment was relieving the guards at Negro Fort, the cannon of Fort Independence thundered. One ball came hurtling through the air toward the earthen redoubt, and one American was killed.

The weather, which had been fairly mild for that time of year, suddenly became worse on January 25th. It became very stormy. The torrential rain caused the Bronx River suddenly to rise over its banks and over the roadway at Williams's Bridge.

The changed conditions of the battlefield caused by the weather undoubtedly emboldened the defenders of Fort Independence. The Americans had no opportunity to complete permanent barracks to shelter themselves from the storm. Some gunpowder got wet and was rendered useless. Moreover, the muddy terrain could only hamper the movement of troops carrying heavy baggage and a few large cannon against a light, mobile force whose source of supply was safely stored in a strong fort. Thus, early in the morning of January 25th, the fort's defenders sallied out beyond the walls in a successful attempt to rout American units Heath had stationed at DeLancey's Mills.

This action emboldened the Hessian commander to make a strong thrust toward Isaac Valentine's house at 10 o'clock in the morning. The garrison, constantly firing, poured out of Fort Independence, driving the American guards from Negro Fort and from the stone house. As the Hessians passed over the hill, some of their fire reached beyond the Bronx River to John Williams's house. The retreating Americans fled for safety to the old redoubt overlooking Williams's Bridge, while their pursuers lined up behind one of Isaac Valentine's stone walls that divided his fields near the base of the hill, just to the southwest. Two American militia regiments had managed to flee across the flooded Williams's Bridge and grouped there. Heath noticed that with them were field cannon already harnessed to horses, and the general ordered Captain Lieutenant Bryant to ford the flooded bridge with one such piece, bringing a party of militiamen to provide protective cover. The maneuver was successful, and Bryant urged the horses to pull the cannon up the crest of the hill. Fearing that the horses might be shot if he should expose them to the danger, Bryant unharnessed them from the cannon and had his men take the ropes to drag the field piece over the top of the hill to a position on the other slope where it could be settled and trained on the stone wall from behind which the Hessians were firing. So close was it, that it was almost in range of a pistol shot. Bryant had the cannon shoot one ball which opened up a breach in the stone wall four or five feet (about a little more than one to one and a half meters) wide. Stunned, the Hessians did not move. Quickly, Bryant brought off a second shot, and this caused the Hessians to flee back to Fort Independence. For the second time in eight days, Isaac Valentine's farm was a battleground.

Despite the failure of the Hessian sally, Heath knew that he did not have enough cannon to continue the siege, an estimate which the defenders inside Fort Independence and the British army in New York City undoubtedly shared. No relief column was sent to aid the defenders, so the American effort at creating a diversion was a failure. All attempts to draw out the guard at the fort once again were unsuccessful.

On January 29th, rapidly lowering clouds presaged the onset of a severe snowstorm. All the American generals on the expedition agreed it was prudent to withdraw before it came. The only object of Heath's foray into the King's Bridge area that could still be attempted was to carry off and destroy the British forage, but the situation there was too dangerous for that. It was decided that this object could be pursued at a position farther to the north where the troops could have permanent barracks. Consequently, just after sundown, in the midst of a heavy snowfall, the American troops were ordered back along the same routes they had used when they first came.[53]

As the American troops trudged back past the stone farmhouse, and as the last of the American rear guard at Negro Fort and at the house itself followed their comrades northward,

Isaac Valentine probably had mixed emotions. He would be relieved that he had survived two battles fought on his own property, although he would be left with their wreckage. If he knew about the American object of taking forage, he might also have been relieved that the troops had no opportunity to take whatever livestock and grain he had left from previous attempts on them by both sides. Yet, there might have been a tinge of apprehension as well. The Americans were leaving his land for a second time, leaving him at the mercy of the British, the Tories, and the Hessians once again. Moreover, Valentine knew that the King's Bridge was a major military target. It was possible that more attacks on Fort Independence would be made, and he would have to undergo the ordeal of war another time.

Indeed, in February, there were two more attempts at Fort Independence, a stronger one on February 6th and a minor one on February 10th, but Isaac Valentine and his farm were not involved in either.[54] Nevertheless, circumstances at Valentine's house in that month were such that he had to be extremely careful.

In February, 1777, Colonel Robert Rogers, the Tory commander of the green-coated Queen's Rangers, occupied Isaac Valentine's stone house. Already despised by ardent American patriots for his leading role as a Tory, he was warmly opposed by those farmers from whom he had taken grain and livestock for the use of his and the British troops. Rogers eagerly returned these sentiments, ever on the alert to ensnare anyone who was a rebel, such as Marcus Christian of Eastchester.

Marcus Christian's neighbor was Thomas Fowler, who frequently drove his own cattle and hogs down the Boston Post Road past Isaac Valentine's house to sell at the market in New York City. One early February day, Christian noticed his neighbor had stolen two cows from him to drive with the Fowler herd. When Christian protested, Fowler told him he could whistle for his cattle, and took them anyway. A few days later, on February 6th, Fowler, accompanied by three British light horsemen, accused Christian of being a rebel, arrested him, and dragged him to Isaac Valentine's house to confront

1774–1777: YEAR OF BATTLE

Robert Rogers used the Valentine House as a headquarters in February, 1777. *The Bettmann Archive.*

Colonel Rogers. There, Fowler told Rogers that his neighbor was a spy, and the commander of the Rangers, facing Christian, announced that the hapless prisoner would be hanged. Perhaps the speed with which Rogers considered the matter was colored by the attack on nearby Fort Independence occurring at the same time. Nevertheless, Christian was thrown into one of the rooms of the house, called by some the provost, the name also used for the jail in New York City, and by others, the guard house. There, he spent nine anxious days until February 15th, when he was able to escape. He was eventually picked up by an American patrol.[55]

Nevertheless, the principal danger to Isaac Valentine, his house and his farm, was from military action. In March, the main object of American thrusts into the vicinity was still to obtain provisions for the troops by forage, thus denying them to the British. On the morning of March 16, 1777, 40 Americans, accompanied by five or six teams of horses, started down from Eastchester to Morrisania on such a mission. Ahead were 40 more men commanded by Captain Samuel Delavan to scout for them and to cover their operation. A picket from Fort Independence, probably composed of members of the Rangers, moving along the Boston Post Road past the stone farmhouse spotted the American scouts moving southward on the east side of the Bronx River at Williams's Bridge and attacked them. Some members of the picket, re-enforced by nearby troops that raised their total to about fifty, took shelter in the redoubt overlooking the bridge and kept firing upon the American scouts across the Bronx River, who answered in a like manner. Meanwhile, the foraging party skirted the fighting to continue its mission. The constant report of musket fire kept up until late afternoon, when the scouts on the east bank of the river were joined by the American foraging party returning from Morrisania. The Americans retreated northward.[56] For the third time, Isaac Valentine's farm had been turned into a battlefield.

As the snows of winter melted and the trees sprouted buds, Isaac Valentine and his neighbors attempted to resume their normal lives. The fields had to be planted; the remaining livestock had to be grazed; the few cows had to be milked. To perform these tasks was no mere desire. It was a matter of survival.

As the glories of spring made way for the heat of summer, Valentine might have wanted to blot out the memory of the harrowing experiences of the earlier part of the year. However, the constant military patrols of the Hessians, Tories, and British were there to remind him. So, too, were the occasional American thrusts at Fort Independence, producing sporadic musket fire, such as happened on June 12th. Also, there were raids performed by Tories to steal provisions from the American encampments in the upper part of Westchester County. For instance, on the night of June 29th, British Major Grant, leading some New York Volunteers, dashed up to White Plains and returned the evening of the following day with eight prisoners, 25 cattle and eleven horses. As soon as he arrived, Colonel Stephen DeLancey set off with another party, coming back after nightfall on July 1st bearing 25 prisoners and 20 cattle.[57]

It was obvious that distant events would affect Isaac Valentine and his affairs. On June 10th, Sir William Howe named General Sir Henry Clinton to command the posts in the New York area, including King's Bridge, in his absence.[58] Howe planned to move a large portion of his army down to Philadelphia. After he did so, Clinton started to amass a large number of troops at King's Bridge in August prior to an attempt to move up the Hudson to support another British army under General John Burgoyne moving down from Canada.

With the fortifications around King's Bridge beginning to overflow with men, Joe, an 18-year old yellow-complexioned slave belonging to Isaac Valentine, used the opportunity to run off on August 2nd. He traveled lightly taking no baggage and carrying nothing that would impede his progress. Wearing only homespun clothes, he had nothing that could distinguish him from others, except, perhaps, for a sleeveless red jacket. Although Joe had been brought up in nearby West Farms, it was not likely that he returned there. Valentine spent nine full days inquiring after him from people in the neighborhood, but in the end, he had to advertise his loss, offering 40 shillings reward for Joe's return.[59] It is not known whether Isaac Valentine ever got him back.

It is also doubtful whether Valentine's blacksmith business flourished after his farm became a battlefield. The bustling traffic on the Boston Post Road in front of his house dwindled to a trickle and almost ended altogether. The raids on the farms in the county by supporters of both sides brought many of his customers to ruin. These raids had a terrifying effect on their personalities, making them fearful and apathetic. Why bother to repair anything when, after all, it will be destroyed in the next raid? In later years, Timothy Dwight, who was a chaplain in the Continental Army and subsequently President of Yale, recalled the scene he beheld in the area in the autumn of 1777:

> The unhappy inhabitants were . . . actually plundered. They feared every body whom they saw and loved nobody. It was . . . melancholy . . . to hear their conversation. To every question they gave such an answer as would please the inquirer; or . . . such a one as would not provoke him. Fear apparently was the only passion by which they were animated. . . . They were not civil, but obsequious; not obliging but subservient. . . . Both their countenances and motions had lost every trace of animation and feeling. Their features were smooth, not in serenity, but apathy; . . . and all thought, beyond what was merely instinctive, had fled their minds forever.
> Their houses, in the meantime, were in a great measure scenes of desolation. Their furniture was extensively plundered or broken to pieces. The walls, floors and windows were injured, both by violence and decay, and were not repaired because they had no means to repair them, and because they were exposed to the repetition of the same injuries. Their cattle were gone. Their enclosures were burnt when they were capable of becoming fuel, and in many

cases thrown down when they were not. Their fields were covered with a rank outgrowth of weeds and wild grass.

Amid all this desolation, nothing struck my eye more forcibly than the sight of this great road the passage from New York to Boston. Where I had heretofore seen a continual succession of horses and carriages, life and bustle . . . not a single, solitary traveller was seen, from week to week or from month to month. The world was motionless and silent, except when one of these unhappy people ventured upon a rare and lonely excursion to the house of a neighbor no less unhappy; or a scouting party, traversing the country in quest of enemies, alarmed the inhabitants with expectations of new injuries and sufferings. The very tracks of the carriages were grown over and obliterated, and, when they were discernable, resembled faint impressions. . . . The grass was of full height for the scythe. . . .[60]

These conditions were aggravated by the fury of the raids carried on by Tories led by Colonel James DeLancey, who had been the last sheriff of Westchester County chosen by the colonial government. On October 5th, this avid British partisan led his light horsemen from King's Bridge to White Plains and brought back flour, oxen, cattle, sheep, and hogs.[61] Eventually, the inhabitants were to call DeLancey's men "Cowboys" because of all the cattle they stole. Depredations of equal effect were caused by partisan American units descending upon farms from upper Westchester County. People thought that, figuratively, they would be skinned alive by them to prevent the British from obtaining any provisions or benefit. Consequently, these American foragers were eventually called "Skinners." The depredations by both sides were kept up year after year until the war was over.

Yet, in 1777, the war still raged, and Isaac Valentine and his house were on the front line. By early November, Sir Henry Clinton's thrust up the Hudson had come to nought, and Burgoyne's army in upper New York State had been captured at Saratoga, handing the British a stunning defeat. The 2,500 defenders of the King's Bridge were now frightened and withdrew from their far-flung outposts to collect all their strength at the bridge. A significant number of Hessians and Queen's Rangers deserted to the Americans, bringing with them the rumor that Fort Independence was to be abandoned.[62]

Major General Israel Putnam, who now commanded the American troops in the area, believed a thrust at King's Bridge might be successful. He especially wanted to capture James DeLancey at West Farms. With 4,000 men, Putnam advanced down to Williams's Bridge on the evening of November 28th. He then sent an advance party of 300 foot soldiers, 100 horsemen, some cannon and mortars across the Bronx River, down the Boston Post Road past Isaac Valentine's house toward Fort Independence. Suddenly, they were faced with a picket of 47 men led by Captain Andreas Emmerich, a German who had previously settled in America and had raised his own corps in Germany to fight for the British. Later, Irishmen and American Tories also joined the unit. Emmerich's corps were chasseurs, soldiers especially trained and equipped for rapid action.

The training of these chasseurs was now put to the test. Opening fire on the slower moving Americans, they caused the advance party to retreat, once again passing Isaac Valentine's house, toward Williams's Bridge and the safety of the large force on the other side. To prevent Emmerich's men from following them by crossing the bridge, Putnam ordered a cannon to fire at the pursuers on Valentine's farm, thus causing the chasseurs to retreat and to allow the Americans peaceably to withdraw. Another unit Putnam had dispatched to West Farms did capture James DeLancey,[63] whom they managed to hold for a short while. However, in this engagement, Valentine's farm served as a battlefield for the fourth time in one year. It would not be the last.

On December 15, 1777, a party of Americans, probably on a foraging mission, came from upper Westchester County to Williams's Bridge. While some remained on the east bank of

Israel Putnam commanded American troops in an engagement involving Isaac Valentine's house in November, 1777. Engraving by W. Humphreys after a sketch by John Trumbull. *Courtesy of The New-York Historical Society.*

the Bronx River, about 150 crossed the stream to Isaac Valentine's farm. Twenty American dragoons and fifty infantrymen immediately occupied the stone house and the land near it, and three dragoons pressed forward to Negro Fort. Captain

Emmerich, near Fort Independence, spotted the three men in the earthen redoubt and ordered his riflemen to investigate. As the riflemen approached, the men at Valentine's farmhouse noticed them and opened fire on the chasseurs, who quickly attacked. About 100 of the men on the farm swiftly ran back to Williams's Bridge, followed closely by those who were defending the house. Because of the suddenness of the chasseurs' attack and the precipitate flight across the river, the Americans were thrown into utter confusion and could not make a stand at the bridge. The chasseurs kept up the chase for about a mile (just over 1½ kilometers) when Captain Emmerich himself caught up with his men. With a keen eye, he observed that there were American troops which had remained on the east bank of the river while the others had gone to the Valentine farm. Emmerich suspected a trap, and ordered his men to break off contact with the Americans, to cross the Bronx River again, re-pass Isaac Valentine's house, and seek the safety of their own lines at King's Bridge.[64]

Thus, in the space of one year, Valentine's farm was the scene of five military engagements. Indeed, 1777 could have been called justifiably by the blacksmith as the year of battle. Undoubtedly, Isaac Valentine was relieved that this trying year was ending. However, as he and his neighbors were aware, the war was not yet over.

CHAPTER FIVE

1778–1783: Years of Peril

With the lower part of New York State apparently firmly in British possession (the Americans holding onto the northern edge of Westchester County as their front line), in 1778, the British authorities took an inventory of the houses and farms of all the known rebels from those quarters. In the town of Westchester, only four rebels were listed in Fordham, including the deceased Continental general, Richard Montgomery, whose heirs presumably inherited the property. Also on the list were Richard Morris, brother of General Lewis Morris, signer of the Declaration of Independence, and Isaac Valentine's neighbor, John Peter Tetard, and the captain of Valentine's erstwhile militia company, Nicholas Berrian.[65] However, Valentine himself was not considered a rebel at all, since he remained in quiet possession of his property and he did not take up arms against the British army. As he had suffered in silence throughout 1777 when his property became a battlefield several times, so he had to maintain silence in the perilous years of British occupation that followed if he were to have any chance of maintaining ownership of his stone house and his farm.

To appear to remain neutral in the conflict was not easy. Nearby King's Bridge was still an important strategic point and would continue to be an American military objective to the end of the war. Consequently, it was necessary for the British to protect this vital approach to New York in sheer defense. Thus, the neighborhood surrounding Isaac Valentine's stone house would be constantly swarming with troops.

In the spring of 1778, Andreas Emmerich was promoted to lieutenant colonel and established his headquarters in John

Peter Tetard's vacant house between Valentine's home and the King's Bridge. The Queen's Rangers, now under the command of Lieutenant Colonel John Graves Simcoe, joined Emmerich's corps and a number of other Tory units to defend the area. Fort Independence was garrisoned with Hessians. To show these troops the importance attached to their position, on April 27th, General Sir Henry Clinton and his staff came to King's Bridge from New York and passed along the lines of Fort Independence, arriving at Emmerich's headquarters. Clinton observed a sham battle, which showed him the state of the troops' readiness. He then examined the redoubts in the area, probably including the two on Isaac Valentine's farm, and then reviewed the Tory troops before returning to New York.[66]

However, in wartime, military activity is not confined to sham battles, inspections and colorful reviews. That spring, a number of small American patrols did advance as far as Williams's Bridge, and for one night in the middle of July after a skirmish in Yonkers, a grand guard of the Queen's Rangers was marched past Isaac Valentine's house to man the redoubt overlooking the crossing. In the morning, the troops retraced their steps back to their previous position.[67]

Near the end of August, a band of Stockbridge Indians with an American scouting party was approaching the outer edges of the area patrolled by the King's Bridge garrison (near today's Bronx–Yonkers line) on Mile Square Road. Both Simcoe and Emmerich were then in Eastchester on the east banks of the Bronx River. A plan was made for the Hessians to ambush the Indians, and to perform his part, Simcoe had to move to his left, cross Williams's Bridge onto Isaac Valentine's farm and turn northward up Mile Square Road. On August 31, 1778, the Stockbridge Indians were caught in the trap, and most were killed.[68]

In 1778, France entered the war on the American side, and the British, in an attempt to conserve their resources to meet the danger from their age-old adversary, vainly tried to achieve peace with their rebellious colonists by offering them freedom from taxation. This offer was rejected by all American officials because it fell short of granting independence. However, the British tried to appeal over the heads of the officials directly to the people by printing the offer in a royal proclamation. On October 14th, copies of the printed proclamation were delivered to the garrison at King's Bridge, and parties were sent out to post them on all the houses in the vicinity.[69] Undoubtedly, one was posted on Isaac Valentine's house. Nevertheless, the proclamation had no effect, and the war continued.

By early November, the British army was making preparations for going into winter quarters. To do so, the Hessians and Tories comprising the King's Bridge garrison advanced north and eastward, fanning out past Isaac Valentine's farm, to protect thousands of workers and about a hundred wagons used in demolishing the houses of the rebels in Yonkers and Eastchester. The material would be used to build huts for the soldiers. After this work was completed on November 5th, Colonel Simcoe had discovered that there were not enough huts at King's Bridge to house all the regiments there. He suggested to Major General William Tryon, once the royal governor of New York, that some houses in Eastchester be destroyed to make up the deficiency, and to use the opportunity also to capture American militia colonel Thomas Thomas. Tryon approved, and on November 13th, Simcoe, Emmerich, and the men under their commands, marched past Isaac Valentine's house on their mission. Colonel Thomas was captured, and Tryon, who arrived later to observe the demolition, was able to return over the same road with fifty loads of doors, windows, lumber and fittings. With this haul, the army moved into its winter quarters.[70]

Valentine's house escaped demolition for several reasons. It was located neither in Yonkers nor in Eastchester, the twin targets of the effort. Moreover, the house was made of stone, rather than of wood, the material needed for building barracks. Considering all this, undoubtedly the structure survived because the blacksmith continued to live there without expressing support for the American cause.

However, the army had to be fed, and enterprising men near American-held Rye secretly purchased cattle from the farmers there, hid them in the woods and at out of the way places for the night, slipped them by the American guards and drove them down the Boston Post Road past Isaac Valentine's house to New York. This practice was not stopped even when a corps of 4,000 men under British Quartermaster General Sir William Erskine crossed the King's Bridge in early December, 1778, in a vain attempt to dash to Peekskill to rescue Burgoyne's entire army, which had been made prisoners of war after the battle of Saratoga. While this maneuver was under way, a Captain Olmstead from Colonel Enos's Connecticut Regiment was on his way from Horseneck (modern Greenwich, Connecticut) to New York under a flag of truce. The American captain was not permitted to continue his journey while the military operation was in progress to prevent him from observing anything which might provide the rebels with information. Therefore, Olmstead was detained for several days in Isaac Valentine's house. Nevertheless, while there, he did observe 200 head of cattle and a great number of sheep and hogs pass by. Once his mission was completed, Olmstead reported his observations, and the Americans increased their security measures.[71]

It is probably because of this that, at four o'clock in the morning of February 25, 1779, General Tryon, accompanied by British and Tory regiments and Emmerich's chasseurs, marched past Isaac Valentine's house to attack the Americans at Horseneck to obtain food for the troops, returning on February 27th at four o'clock in the afternoon. A month later, on March 25th, Tryon led 1,500 men over the same road on the same mission, encountering an American reconnoitering party of 30 in New Rochelle and chasing them back to Connecticut.[72]

However, it was not until the end of May that the British put a major plan into motion, attempting to capture American fortifications at Teller's and Verplanck's Points in upper Westchester County, and Stony Point on the west bank of the Hudson. As a first step toward this goal, on May 28th, the British Tory and Hessian troops guarding the King's Bridge in upper Manhattan and on the mainland marched out in four columns advancing to Yonkers. Several units were encamped on Isaac Valentine's farm, while others were posted at Williams's Bridge with their tents.[73]

While this maneuver was under way, a rumor (which eventually proved to be true) began to circulate among the troops that the British commanders had decided to break up Emmerich's chasseurs, dividing the men among existing units and providing the officers with positions as they became available. As with any military organization, the troops had developed a camaraderie, and it is most likely that it was they who were the instigators of a curious certificate that was handed to Colonel Emmerich on June 27, 1779. The certificate purports to be from a number of Tories and those not supporting the British government saying that Emmerich had protected their persons and properties, and that it would be a misfortune if he were ordered away on another service.[74] It is difficult to believe that such a document originated freely from the populace of the area considering the widespread depredations that the chasseurs and other Tory units had committed. Moreover, the certificate was dated at the camp Emmerich's corps was occupying, not at the home of any of the signers. The document was signed by 70 men living in Yonkers, Eastchester, Fordham and Westchester. Conspicuously absent is the name of Isaac Valentine, who lived on the farm adjoining Emmerich's headquarters in Tetard's house, and who often had to play host to the chasseurs on patrol. Its absence is an indication of the untruths in the certificate's statements. If it is true that Emmerich's men had originated the document and had urged the residents to sign it, the lack of Valentine's signature is eloquent testimony of the blacksmith's courage and mute evidence of his political sympathies.

As it developed, however, the British thrust at the American forts was dealt a mortal blow when General Anthony Wayne of the Continental Army recaptured Stony Point on July 15, 1779. Sir Henry Clinton was convinced his plan could not succeed, and ordered his troops to return. Two days later, 250 men were deployed between King's Bridge and Mamaroneck to gather hay to supply all the horses in the British garrison through the winter.[75] Undoubtedly, one place on which they worked was Isaac Valentine's farm. By July 31st, all of the British, Tory and Hessian troops had marched back over the King's Bridge, except Emmerich's corps, which manned the mainland fortifications, and the Tory major, Mansfield Bearmore, who led a detachment of James DeLancey's notorious "Cowboys" stationed near Fort Number Eight (today's Bronx Community College campus).[76]

On August 5th, the Hessians received information that an American party was marching to attack. Major Bearmore, and the Tory troops of the British Legion, Simcoe's Rangers and Emmerich's corps, joined by Captain Ernst Friedrich von Diemar's Hussars, dashed up the Boston Post Road, past Isaac Valentine's house, over Williams's Bridge, to intercept it. They caught up to the Americans between New Rochelle and Mamaroneck, and ended this threat.[77]

Nevertheless, Sir Henry Clinton was so discouraged by British prospects in the vicinity that he had resolved to conserve his forces in New York in order to deploy more troops in other theatres of the war. In this light, the fortifications north of King's Bridge were expendable, while the works defending the crossing on the Manhattan side would have to be strengthened. Labor on this project began in the second week of August. On August 16th, all the guns were removed from Fort Independence and transferred to forts in Manhattan. The woodwork was similarly removed the following day and carried over in wagons. By September 12th, work began on demolishing the fort itself, and six days later, the remains of its powder magazine were destroyed.[78]

However, such work did not end the usual need of the army to find food for the oncoming winter. Consequently, on September 6th, troops from the King's Bridge posts set out along the Boston Post Road, past Isaac Valentine's house, to raid Horseneck, where they carried off cattle, sheep, poultry, and other provisions to New York.[79]

On the night of October 2, 1779, as the demolition of the mainland forts was nearing completion, a patrol of Maryland dragoons under Lieutenant Erasmus Gill was marching southward from Eastchester. A small detachment of British infantry with some of von Diemar's Hussars was sent along the Boston Post Road and over Williams's Bridge to attempt to ambush the Americans. At daybreak, a Hessian Jäger corps under Captain Johann Ewald followed, crossing the bridge to protect the rear of the first party. A Jäger picket under Alexander Wilhelm Bickell remained on the Valentine farm, on the west bank of the Bronx River just north of the road. For all the planning, the ambush went awry when the Marylanders took a route other than what was expected. However, Lieutenant Gill was captured, and he was taken back past Isaac Valentine's house in the custody of Captain Ewald.[80]

By November 7th, only the camp of Colonel Ludwig Johann Adolph von Wurmb's Hessians remained to defend the King's Bridge from the mainland side. With the post in such weakened condition, there existed an inviting situation whereby daring American commanders could raid as far south as Morrisania with little chance of discovery or battle. One of these was a French nobleman, Charles Trefin, Marquis de la Rouaire, who became a colonel in the American army using the name Charles Armand. He was determined to capture the notorious Tory "Cowboy" Major Bearmore at Oak Point on the Hunts Point peninsula. Marching from Tarrytown to Eastchester, he reached Williams's Bridge on the morning of November 7th. There, he posted some of his infantry. Advancing 100 yards (about 90 meters) onto Isaac Valentine's farm, he positioned the rest behind some of the stone walls that separated one field from another. All this was to secure his retreat in case von Wurmb discovered the operation. With 20 dragoons, Armand then galloped to Oak Point, snatched Bearmore, fell back to the Valentine farm, and recrossed Williams's Bridge without once alerting the Hessians camped within two miles (just over 3 kilometers) of his presence.[81]

Eight days later, on November 15th, the troops under British command moved into their winter quarters, and none remained encamped north of the King's Bridge. This situation, coupled with his previous success, tempted Colonel Armand to use the same plan to capture the leader of the "Cowboys," Colonel James DeLancey, who was headquartered at Richard Morris's house in Fordham (today, near the Bronx Community College campus). On December 1, 1779, Armand once again stationed his troops near Williams's Bridge, and galloped

LEGACY OF THE REVOLUTION

toward the Morris house, but DeLancey had escaped his grasp by being in New York at the time. Snatching Isaac Corsa instead, Armand once more returned to the Valentine farm, and retreated to the American lines.[82]

Armand's two raids signalled the beginning of a subtle change in the nature of the military operations that would occur in the vicinity of Isaac Valentine's house in the ensuing years. While the strategic King's Bridge would continue to be a military objective, the absence of a permanent garrison on the mainland side of the crossing meant that the American troops did not have to exercise their previous caution in approaching Williams's Bridge. Moreover, with no bar to stop them from going further, the Valentine farm became just another property raiding parties had to dash across to reach more distant goals. Connected with this was the vulnerability of Isaac Valentine's crops and livestock to plunder from both sides. Heretofore, whichever side in the conflict manned the nearby forts could easily claim Valentine's produce and meat, while successfully deterring raiding parties of the other side from venturing so close to its fortifications. With the forts demolished, there was little to hinder army groups or roving bands of "Cowboys" or "Skinners" from distant places from swooping down upon the Valentine farm and carrying away any valuable movable property.

In the light of this changed situation, on December 16th, thirty Americans dashed from Tarrytown to Morrisania and West Farms across Isaac Valentine's farm to grab some horses and to take some Tories prisoner. On the morning of December 17th, Tory Colonel Hatfield, headquartered in Richard Morris's house, set out to pursue the raiding party with a detachment of "Cowboys." Passing across the Valentine farm, he caught up with them in Tuckahoe, re-took the horses and the prisoners, and returned.[83]

As a counterstroke, on January 18, 1780, an American militia party commanded by Captain Lockwood advanced from Horseneck, across Williams's Bridge, past Isaac Valentine's stone house, to the Morris house, besieged it and burned it to the ground. When the party retreated across Williams's

Bridge, the "Cowboys" regrouped and pursued it, but the damage had been done.[84]

Meanwhile, the official policy of the British military authorities was to encourage the farmers in the area to raise supplies of forage, grain, and vegetables for army use and to protect them from any depredation. Nevertheless, this policy did not deter small groups of Hessians, British, or Tories from harming or destroying stock, produce, houses, or farms. The situation got to be so bad that, in March, Hessian General Knyphausen, then the commanding officer in the region, officially placed all farmers in the area under his protection and warned that those committing the depredations would be punished severely. He also encouraged those farmers with a grievance to complain to the nearest military post.[85]

Knyphausen's declaration did not appear to change the situation. In the summer of 1780, when American Brigadier General John Stark led a foraging expedition with 200 wagons from North Castle over Williams's Bridge and the Valentine farm to West Farms, Dr. James Thatcher, a surgeon who accompanied him, described a scene bleaker than that beheld by Timothy Dwight just three years earlier:

> The country is rich and fertile, and the farms appear to have been advantageously cultivated, but now it has the marks of a country in ruins. A large proportion of the proprietors having abandoned their farms, and the few that remain, find it impossible to harvest the produce. The meadows and pastures are covered with grass of a summers growth, and thousands of bushels of apples and other fruit, are rotting in the orchards.[86]

Perhaps it was to deter such expeditions as this that once again Hessian Jägers were encamped temporarily near the old Fort Independence near the end of July.[87]

When winter winds once again swept across the bleak farmlands near King's Bridge, American Lieutenant Colonel William Hull planned a major expedition against Colonel

James DeLancey's "Cowboys." Descending from Pine's Bridge to Williams's Bridge along Mile Square Road on January 21, 1781, he began to deploy his force. Captain Maxwell was sent past Isaac Valentine's house with his 100 men to hold down the British garrison at Fort Number Eight. Another company was sent to West Farms and a third to Throg's Neck. Two companies remained to guard Williams's Bridge to keep the line of retreat open. The expedition was a success. Hull's men took 50 prisoners, 60 horses, and a number of cattle.[88]

However, it was not until July, 1781, that Isaac Valentine's farm once again became a battlefield. George Washington was encamped in upper Westchester County, awaiting a junction with the French army under the command of the Comte de Rochambeau marching toward him. Washington saw this as an opportunity to attack New York City, but to carry it out, he needed two things—accurate information about the strength and position of the British forces and the elimination of the military power of Colonel James DeLancey's "Cowboys" on the mainland.

To combat the "Cowboys," Washington secured the aid of the Duc de Lauzun, commander of a French legion of cavalry and infantry, assisted by some American troops. This mixed force was to sweep down from Eastchester to capture DeLancey and his men. It was planned that when he reached Williams's Bridge, the Duc would send an officer and an escort across Isaac Valentine's farm to communicate with American troops sent down from upper Westchester County to achieve Washington's other objective.

This American force, commanded by Major General Benjamin Lincoln, was to come down the Hudson River in rowboats at night, land in northern Manhattan, and to try to coax the garrisons defending the forts there out into the open to ascertain their number. If he could safely capture any, he was ordered to do so. Otherwise, he was to retreat across the King's Bridge for safety. If Lincoln determined that he could not land in Manhattan, he was to post himself on the heights above King's Bridge to act in concert with the Duc de Lauzun to prevent any of DeLancey's men from escaping from the mainland to the protection of the island forts.

On the night of July 2, 1781, Lincoln and his men determined it was safer to land in Yonkers, and the Americans were deployed to aid the French commander in his mission. Before daylight on July 3rd, he occupied the ground near the ruins of Fort Independence. One detachment was stationed on Vault Hill behind the Van Cortlandt house.

At about the same time Lincoln was landing in Yonkers, Lieutenant Colonel Emmerich had led 100 men in that direction on a routine patrol. At 10 o'clock in the evening of July 2nd, the British garrison received word that General Washington's army was moving down from Sing Sing (today's Ossining), thus placing Emmerich in danger. To recall him, a detachment under Hessian Lieutenant Colonel Ernst Carl von Prueschenck crossed the King's Bridge near daybreak of July 3rd. The Hessian commander was cautious enough not to pass under the steep hill holding the ruins of Fort Independence, and he sent an advance guard ahead of him, and a party of a sergeant and ten men to examine the fort and its environs.

Meanwhile, DeLancey's "Cowboys" at Fort Number Eight had received word of the mission of the Duc de Lauzun from a deserter. Independently of von Prueschenck, they marched to Isaac Valentine's farm, taking position among the trees west of Williams's Bridge to meet the French cavalry once it crossed the Bronx River. Colonel James DeLancey established his headquarters in Negro Fort.

Thus, at dawn of July 3, 1781, the scene near King's Bridge was peculiar. Hessian Colonel von Prueschenck and his men were in the valley north of the bridge on a rescue mission. A sergeant and ten men were scaling the steep hill on the east to the ruins of Fort Independence. Atop the hill on the plain to the eastward, American General Lincoln's troops were arrayed. Unknown to them, about a mile and a half (almost 2½ kilometers) to their rear, on Isaac Valentine's farm, facing away from them and towards Williams's Bridge, were DeLancey's men awaiting the forces under the Duc de Lauzun.

When the sergeant finally reached the top of the hill near Fort Independence, he squinted at the soldiers in front of him in the dim light of the dawn, with the rays of the sun in his eyes. He first thought they were Hessian troops, but some anxious Americans seized him. Squirming away, he ran down the hill, giving the alarm. Some Americans opened fire, thus alerting the troops below. In the ensuing battle, the Americans protected themselves by advancing to the ruins of Fort Independence, while von Prueschenck occupied the ruins of John Peter Tetard's house. A combination of cavalry and the Hessian Jägers under Colonel von Wurmb joined the fighting, stopping the American advance and pushing the Continental troops out of the fort's ruins toward the Mile Square Road. Another unit pushed the Americans off Vault Hill toward Williams's Bridge.

The sounds of the battle reached all the way to Eastchester, where the Duc de Lauzun was proceeding on his mission. Perceiving that Lincoln's men would need assistance, the Duc urged his cavalry forward, galloped across Williams's Bridge onto Isaac Valentine's farm, only to be met with withering fire from DeLancey's men. Since the "Cowboys" were firing from behind trees, a cavalry charge was useless, and the Duc was forced to recross the Bronx River for safety.

However, developments did not favor the British side. The Hessian advance from King's Bridge pushing the Americans back forced the left (southernmost) wing of the Continental forces onto Isaac Valentine's farm to the vicinity of the stone house. DeLancey's "Cowboys" suddenly discovered they were in danger of being cut off, since they were sandwiched between the French cavalry in front of them and the American infantry to their rear. To save his men, Colonel James DeLancey ordered a withdrawal. This allowed the Duc de Lauzun to cross Williams's Bridge again to aid the American left wing on the Valentine farm. The Hessians soon spotted the French cavalry and estimated their opposition now had superior numbers. Moreover, behind the Americans stood Valentine's woods, and the Hessians, familiar with the native tactics of hiding among foliage, could not be sure if more troops were hidden there. This, coupled with the knowledge that Washington was still moving southward with the main American army, caused the Hessians to fall back to their original position, leaving only a small unit in the ruins of Fort Independence to observe Washington's arrival in the afternoon and his preliminary reconnoitering of the Manhattan fortifications. That evening, after moving his army northward, the American commander thanked de Lauzun for his aid, and ordered his men and those of Brigadier General David Waterbury to place their pickets for the night along the roads from Eastchester to King's Bridge.[89]

It was only later in the same month, after Washington and Rochambeau had joined their main armies in upper Westchester County, that another operation was put in motion in the vicinity of Isaac Valentine's stone house. The American commander still was set on invading New York, and to do so, he had to gather more information about the British defenses on Manhattan and Long Island. To obtain it, he had to move 5,000 troops down to the area below the present Bronx–Westchester border, clear it of DeLancey's men and reconnoiter the fortifications for two days.

Consequently, on July 22, 1781, at 9 o'clock in the morning, Washington and Rochambeau accompanied the allied forces who arrived marching in columns to where Fort Independence once stood. The division of Brigadier General Samuel Holden Parsons was the first to arrive at the spot, while the Duc de Lauzun's Legion marched from Yonkers to the Valentine farm and then to Williams's Bridge. American and French forces fanned out to occupy the plain between the stone house and the demolished fort, and spread southward to West Farms. At the appointed time, de Lauzun's cavalry dashed away from its post near Williams's Bridge, across Isaac Valentine's farm to Morrisania to participate in the attempt to clear DeLancey's "Cowboys" from the area so that the allied commanders could conduct their reconnaissance without danger. Once the mission was completed, the horsemen returned to the camp at the bridge.

With the exception of Rochambeau's staff and some guards who accompanied the French general and Washington on their observations, all the French troops remained in their camps between the ruins of Fort Independence and the Bronx River to intimidate the garrison in northern Manhattan and at Fort Number Eight. Undoubtedly, many were posted on Isaac Valentine's farm. Unfortunately, the French behaved no better toward the farmers living in the area than the "Cowboys" and "Skinners" who had been ravaging them for years. Their hussars and chasseurs pillaged many houses, and it is likely that Valentine's stone house was one of them.

Rochambeau returned to the French encampment on the Gun Hill late in the evening of July 22nd, bedding down in what was described as "a wretched house." Although it is not certain in which home he slept, the only intact farmhouse standing in that vicinity was Isaac Valentine's. Thus, it is most likely that the French commander slept the night in the stone house by the Boston Post Road.

Near midday of July 23rd, the legion of the Duc de Lauzun was summoned to leave its camp near Williams's Bridge and proceed to Morrisania to help complete the reconnaissance there. The others remained in camp until 5 o'clock in the afternoon when the allied forces had finished their mission and moved northward off the Valentine farm to their previous post in upper Westchester County.[90]

As it turned out, any suffering Isaac Valentine may have undergone by having his farm turned into a battlefield on July 3rd and into a French encampment on July 22nd and 23rd went for nought. Because of developing military circumstances, George Washington dropped his cherished idea of a conquest of New York City, marched his allied troops to Virginia, besieged an entire British army under Lord Cornwallis in Yorktown, and won a decisive victory when the British surrendered on October 19, 1781.

However, the war was not yet over. No truce had been declared and no peace signed. It was not until March 4, 1782, that the British House of Commons voted to end the war. Coincidentally, on the same day, Captain Israel Honeywell, with a body of light horse, galloped down from upper Westchester County, crossing Williams's Bridge onto Isaac Valen-

The Comte de Rochambeau, commander of the French forces in America, may have slept in the Valentine House in July, 1781. *The Bettmann Archive*.

tine's farm, dashing to Morrisania to attack Colonel James DeLancey's camp. As soon as Honeywell rode off to return to his own quarters, the "Cowboys" gathered a number of horses and light infantry to pursue him back across Williams's Bridge. Once on the east bank of the Bronx River, the pursuers ran into an ambush which Honeywell had laid for them, and fighting continued for some time before the "Cowboys" returned to Morrisania.[91]

Isolated incidents occurred in the region while peace negotiations were being conducted in Paris throughout the spring and summer of 1782, but it was evident that the pace of the conflict was slowing down. On May 6th, Sir Guy Carleton arrived in New York to take command of the British army, and on October 20th, Fort Number Eight, the last British fort on the east bank of the Harlem River, was destroyed. Nevertheless, British troops still patrolled the area north of King's Bridge and DeLancey's "Cowboys" were still encamped on the mainland.[92] Isaac Valentine's farm was still in British occupied territory.

On November 5, 1782, British and American diplomats in Paris agreed to a preliminary treaty of peace, which was not signed until January 20, 1783, when France and Spain, two other parties at war with Great Britain, were ready to sign their preliminary treaties. However, it took time for the news to cross the Atlantic, and it was not until March 29th that George Washington joyously announced the coming of peace.[93]

Negotiations were immediately opened between Washington and Sir Guy Carleton on suspending hostilities, which the American commander ordered on April 18, 1783. Attention next turned to the withdrawal of British troops from the territory they occupied. In a rather hasty and ill-considered action, on May 13th, Carleton penned a letter to George Clinton, erstwhile American general now serving as the first governor of New York State, notifying him that the last of the British forces would be withdrawn from Westchester County that day. Clinton did not receive the letter until the 15th, and realized, in horror, that no civil authority had existed in the evacuated area for the previous two days, and that some time would be needed to establish one. The governor quickly requested Richard Morris, who was now the state's chief justice, to rush to Westchester to establish civil government there.[94]

Richard Morris, Chief Justice of New York State, who restored order in the area of the Valentine House following the withdrawal of British troops in May, 1783. Charcoal sketch after Saint Memin. *Courtesy of The New-York Historical Society.*

It was in this period of anarchy lasting about a week that Isaac Valentine's neighbors in the town of Westchester were subjected to one final outburst of fury. Armed bands descended upon the hapless residents, accusing several of being Tories, beating them, robbing them and breaking furniture in their houses. It is likely that Valentine may not have been a victim of these bands. After all, like others in his neighborhood, he remained in peaceful occupation of his lands, had never spoken out against the American side, and had never joined the Tories in the area in taking up arms against the United States. Certainly, he filed no complaint that such depredations were committed against him.[95]

The anarchy ended when Washington, granting a request by Chief Justice Richard Morris, sent the 8th Massachusetts Regiment on May 21st to Mile Square in Yonkers to assist in restoring legal government and to prevent troops from committing any outrages on the inhabitants or their property on the pretext of their being Tories. With their arrival, the depredations immediately ceased.[96]

However, the British still remained in the forts on Manhattan Island, just on the other side of King's Bridge, two miles (just over 3 kilometers) from Isaac Valentine's stone house. The definitive treaty of peace formally ending the war and recognizing the independence of the United States was signed in Paris on September 3, 1783. A month and a half later, Sir Guy Carleton began evacuating Manhattan, and on the morning of November 21st, General Washington crossed the King's Bridge to take possession of the town of Harlem. Four days later, joined by Governor George Clinton, he moved from Harlem to a joyous reception in New York City.[97]

The war was over. It was time for Isaac Valentine and his neighbors to pick up the threads of their lives and to return to the pursuits of peacetime.

CHAPTER SIX

1784-1792: Years of Recovery

The arrival of the blessings of peace temporarily brought an end to Isaac Valentine's anxiety over whether he would be able to preserve his property. Because he had remained in possession of his house and farm, and because he had not taken up arms against either side in the war, his lands were not confiscated by the authorities of the victorious state of New York, as those of Colonel James DeLancey and other British supporters were in the town of Westchester. No one ever accused Valentine of being a Tory.

On the other hand, the six times when his farm served as a battlefield, the innumerable occasions on which it was used as a military encampment, the constant marching of troops and galloping of horses over the fields, the existence of Negro Fort and the redoubt overlooking Williams's Bridge on his farmland, and the use of his stone house for a headquarters and other military purposes did have an adverse effect. Like his neighbors, Isaac Valentine had to repair his buildings, reconstruct the stone walls dividing his fields, and somehow make his farmland, churned up for years by marching men and galloping horses, productive once again.

Valentine had his slaves to aid him in these tasks, but what he lacked was money. Although he remained wealthy in terms of the value of the land, it appears that he had little cash. One way he could obtain money was by raising wheat, the state's chief cash crop, which was milled into flour and exported. However, events beyond Isaac Valentine's control conspired to deny him the benefits he might have expected.

With the end of the war, there suddenly appeared on the

scene an insect which layed its eggs in the young wheat, and whose hatching larvae fed upon the plant, thus destroying it. Mistakenly believing that the Hessians had inadvertently brought it from Europe with them, the farmers began calling the pest the Hessian fly. By the summer of 1784, the Hessian fly had infested the crop on Long Island and Westchester County, almost totally destroying the wheat. Moreover, each year, the pest returned, and the plague spread. In 1786, it had destroyed most of the wheat around New York City, and by the following year, it was of such concern that Governor George Clinton brought it to the attention of the state's legislature. The New York Society for the Promotion of Useful Knowledge requested information about the insect, and farmers offered suggestions to foil the onslaught of the Hessian fly ranging from planting a different strain of wheat to sprinkling salt on the crop.[98]

The immediate effect of the Hessian fly on Isaac Valentine and his neighbors was a reduction of the total amount of wheat for sale. At first, this was caused only by the destruction of the crop by the larvae, but in ensuing years, the farmers sought to plant less wheat in an attempt to avoid the ravages of the insect. Under ordinary circumstances, this would cause a rise in wheat prices because of the scarcity. However, the new country was in the midst of a post-war depression, and the price of wheat actually fell from a high of about 9 shillings a bushel (just over 35 liters) on November 11, 1784, to 7 shillings 6 pence on October 10, 1785, to a rock bottom 6 shillings 6 pence on April 6, 1786.[99]

The depression also affected other products Isaac Valentine and his neighbors could sell for cash. Corn sold for 5 shillings a bushel on November 11, 1784, plummeting to a low of 3 shillings 6 pence on November 29th, only to rebound on February 14, 1785, to 4 shillings 3 pence, remaining at that low price through June, 1786.[100] Valentine could drive some beef cattle to New York City where they could be sold, slaughtered and the meat packed in barrels, but the price at which such packed beef sold at New York indicates similar falling prices. From a high of 70 shillings 6 pence a barrel on November 11,

1784, beef prices declined to 70 shillings on November 29th, to 65 shillings on March 21, 1785, to 64 shillings 6 pence on June 19, 1786.[101]

Of course, Isaac Valentine had the advantage of being a blacksmith, and, as soon as his forge was repaired, he could provide the same services as he had before the war, charging fees for them. Unfortunately, his neighbors were suffering from the same economic conditions as he, and it is doubtful that he received much cash. On the other hand, some money might have come from occasional work he provided to travelers along the Boston Post Road.

With the cessation of hostilities, it was natural for the old commercial traffic patterns to assert themselves, and, once again, drovers with their livestock were passing by Isaac Valentine's stone house to get to markets in New York City. Wagons and carts had a more difficult time initially because of the road's state of disrepair. Nevertheless, attempts were made to repair the roadway, and by September, 1784, the inauguration of a stage wagon service was announced that would link Richmond, Virginia, and Boston, Massachusetts, by initiating service over the then-existing gap between New York City and Stratford, Connecticut. Wagons would leave New York every Monday and Thursday, travel over the Boston Post Road past the stone house, arriving in Stratford two days later. The wagons traveling that stage of the trip would then turn around and depart from Stratford for New York City every Wednesday and Saturday using the same route.[102] Nevertheless, by the spring of 1785, the road still was not fully repaired.[103] A full year was to pass before the proprietors of the wagon service could proudly announce to their prospective customers that repair work on the Boston Post Road was completed.[104] Nevertheless, whatever cash Isaac Valentine may have obtained from incidental work for travelers along the road was not enough to keep him from the financial ruin he had sought to avoid by remaining on his farm throughout the American Revolution.

In fact, the only major asset Valentine possessed in those troubled times was the land, which he could either mortgage or sell to produce the cash he needed. The blacksmith had turned to this asset as early as June 2, 1781, one day before the last military engagement was to be fought on his farm, 22 days before Washington and Rochambeau began their two-day reconnaissance of British fortifications in Manhattan, and four and a half months before Cornwallis was to surrender at Yorktown. On that date, the blacksmith borrowed £200 in New York colonial coins (all paper money printed by any authority was then considered worthless) from his second eldest son, Peter Valentine. As collateral, the blacksmith put up a parcel of land he owned in what was then part of the town of Yonkers on the slope near Van Cortlandt's mill pond (today Van Cortlandt Park's lake) plus some nearby salt meadow, promising to pay back the loan in gold or silver with interest on or before June 2, 1782. On June 21st, Isaac Valentine signed over to Peter the deed to the properties as a bond worth £400 to be used if he should default in repayment.[105] His eldest son, Isaac, Jr., acted as witness to this transaction. Considering the military and economic situation in the region in 1782, coupled with the scarcity of gold and silver, it is not surprising that the blacksmith could not repay the loan on the appointed date.

By 1786, the worsening economic conditions forced Peter Valentine to act. He needed the cash himself, and he turned the blacksmith's debt over to Augustus Van Cortlandt for £250 in New York State money, along with the authority to collect the amount due.[106] However, this was only part of Isaac Valentine's troubles over land and debt.

The blacksmith had also borrowed £700 in gold or silver from Thomas Emmons of Yonkers on August 10, 1785, and to secure the loan, Valentine had put up as collateral a strip of almost 130 acres (52 hectares) he owned facing the Hudson River on the Spuyten Duyvil hill, another piece near Van Cortlandt's mill pond, and two nearby salt meadows. Isaac Valentine could not repay this debt either, and, in 1787, Emmons hauled the blacksmith into court before James M. Hughes, Master in Chancery. Hughes ordered the property in question to be sold at public auction at the Merchants Coffee House in

New York City on July 7th to satisfy the debt.[107] However, no one bid on the land at the auction, and the debt remained.

It was then that Thomas Emmons took advantage of the provisions of a state law passed in 1786 to relieve insolvent debtors, such as Isaac Valentine. By this law, the court could order the blacksmith's property sold, but Emmons, as the mortgage holder, could not be considered a creditor unless he signed a petition giving up the mortgage to an assignee for the benefit of Valentine's creditors. The assignee would then have the power to sell the real estate and redeem all the mortgages.[108] Emmons named the Dutch Reformed Church in New York City as the assignee, and another public auction of the property was held at Caleb Hyatt's tavern near the King's Bridge on July 7, 1788.[109] Once again, no one bid on the property. It would not be the last time the church would attempt to sell it.

In addition, it appears that Isaac Valentine had also borrowed money from Frederick Van Cortlandt, who, for a year, took possession of another strip the blacksmith owned in the town of Yonkers facing the Hudson River on Spuyten Duyvil Hill. Since Valentine could not pay back this debt either, Van Cortlandt agreed to take the property as settlement, purchasing its 140 acres (56 hectares) on June 17, 1788, for the nominal sum of 5 shillings.[110] Although this was the first cash the blacksmith had seen from the sale of land, the sum received hardly solved his problem.

Moreover, on February 11, 1785, Valentine had borrowed £250 from Martha Glean, a widow who had once been married to William Tippet of Yonkers and was executrix of his will. As collateral, the blacksmith not only put up 30 acres (12 hectares) of salt meadow at Tippet's Neck in what was then Yonkers, but for the first time offered two tracts of salt marsh of 4 acres (1½ hectares) each from the property in the town of Westchester which he had first purchased in 1758.[111] Undoubtedly, he had difficulty repaying this loan as well.

If this were not enough, nature added to Isaac Valentine's miseries when a hurricane hit the lower Hudson valley on August 19, 1788. In the morning, moderate rain began to fall with a light wind from the southeast, but at 11 o'clock, the center of the storm moved northward just off the coast of New York, heading inland. The winds increased, becoming ever more violent as they shifted from northeast to north, finally, to west at 1 o'clock in the afternoon. In New York City, the sea swelled, overflowing the wharves, pouring into the streets and flooding cellars. Walls seven feet (just over two meters) thick at the Battery were demolished. In the countryside where Valentine lived, creeks were flooded, large oaks were blown down, fruit trees were torn up by their roots, fences were levelled and fields of corn were flattened.[112] It is also likely that the blacksmith's barn was severely damaged by the storm. It is certain that he had a new one built shortly afterward. Thus, when the hurricane had passed, Isaac Valentine was faced with the necessity of repairing the damage to his property, an expense he could ill-afford.

Despite the blacksmith's desperate financial condition, things were not that bleak. There were signs of hope and very real advances. In June and September, 1786, the prices of wheat, corn and beef finally reversed a trend and rose. In fact, wheat prices, probably reflecting the curtailing of production in response to the Hessian fly, returned to their 1785 level by June, 1787. However, by that time, corn prices fell back to their usual level of 4 shillings 3 pence a bushel, and beef in barrels was selling at an all-time low of 60 shillings 6 pence per barrel.[113]

With another hopeful note, in 1787, the new Constitution of the United States was written, and in 1788, it was ratified by the state of New York. Provisions in the document promised to put in order the chaotic financial situation that had existed in the country since its founding.

With the start of the new government in 1789, there was even an opportunity to witness a bit of pageantry, or at least what passed for pageantry in the young republic. On April 20th, John Adams, newly elected Vice President of the United States, was riding along the Boston Post Road on the way to New York City for his inauguration. He was accompanied by the Westchester County Light Horse under the command of Major Pintard of New Rochelle, who had met Adams at the

Connecticut border and had acted as his escort throughout his journey in the county. The new vice president and his escort passed by Isaac Valentine's stone house on their way toward King's Bridge, where Adams was greeted by a military unit from New York City which accompanied him the rest of the way.[114]

Later in the same year, on October 15th, George Washington, now President of the United States, journeyed along the Boston Post Road in the opposite direction to visit the New England states. Accompanied by a retinue of eight, he passed by Isaac Valentine's house in the afternoon, duplicating a trip he first made in 1775 when he was on his way to Cambridge to take command of the American army. Despite the frequent light showers that fell, the president, retaining the keen eye for observation he developed as a surveyor and a general, noted the progress toward recovery that had been made in the area since the end of the war. As a farmer, he questioned fellow agriculturalists along the way to inquire about their crops. He saw that the road was rough and stony, but that the land was fertile, covered with grass and a luxuriant crop of corn intermixed with pumpkins. That evening, he recalled:

> We met four droves of Beef Cattle for the New York Market (about 30 in a drove) some of which were very fine—also a flock of Sheep for the same place. We scarcely passed a farm house that did not abd. in Geese.
> Their Cattle seemed to be of good quality, and their hogs large, but rather long legged. No dwelling house is seen without a Stone or Brick Chimney, and rarely without a shingled roof. . . .
> The . . . farms . . . are . . . separated, as one Inclosure from another also is, by fences of stone, which are indeed easily made, as the country is immensely stoney. Upon enquiry we find their crops of Wheat and Rye have been abundant—though at first they had sown rather sparingly on acct. of the destruction which had of late years been made of that grain by what is called the Hessian fly.[115]

The mood of Isaac Valentine and his neighbors was optimistic. After passing through the harrowing experiences of the war, they saw the same obvious signs of recovery that Washington had noted. The contrast was so evident that, despite the real difficulties they had faced since the cessation of hostilities, it was clear that life was getting better. It was in this mood that Isaac Valentine decided to erect a spacious barn in the Dutch style, probably to replace the old one which was damaged by the 1788 hurricane.[116]

In addition, the blacksmith was still considered a wealthy man. He lived in his stone house with two other people, most likely his youngest son, John, and his daughter-in-law, Elizabeth. Eight slaves helped him care for his extensive farmlands. Indeed, according to the value of his landed property, by 1790, Valentine could be considered among the wealthiest 18½% of the men in the town of Westchester, and among the richest 13½% in the county.[117] Unfortunately, landed wealth was just about all he had.

Isaac Valentine's mounting debt, aggravated by the costs of repairing damages of the war and the hurricane, by the inability to raise much cash through blacksmithing or selling livestock and grain because of low prices, and by the decision to cut back on wheat production to foil the Hessian fly, had led him to borrow large sums of money using his land as collateral. Although he was unable to pay back the loans, until 1788, the amount of land he lost was comparatively minimal.

Hanging over the blacksmith's head were two outstanding debts—one for £400 which Peter Valentine had sold to Augustus Van Cortlandt to collect, and a second for £700 due to Thomas Emmons, who had assigned it to the Dutch Reformed Church in New York. Van Cortlandt had hauled Valentine into the state's Supreme Court, and Chief Justice Richard Morris ordered that the lands in question be seized by the state and sold to recover the £400 the blacksmith owed, plus £14 and 12 shillings in interest, damages, and costs. On December 4, 1788, Westchester County Sheriff Thomas Thomas, erstwhile militia colonel, sold the lands in two parcels. Frederick Van Cortlandt bid the highest for one 60 acre (24 hectare) parcel, paying £246

New York currency for it. Augustus Van Cortlandt bid highest, £142, for the second lot, 10 acres (4 hectares) containing an old orchard.[118]

The debt owed to Thomas Emmons was more serious. Although two attempts had been made to sell the properties in question, no one had attempted to purchase them. The Dutch Reformed Church was determined to collect, and as Isaac Valentine's debts and the interest on them continued to mount, the land that the blacksmith had purchased in 1758 from that same institution and upon which he had built his stone house was placed in jeopardy.

Evidently, the Church had obtained title to Valentine's Fordham Manor property, as well as the land in Yonkers it had previously sought to sell. Together, it amounted to an enormous 500 acres (200 hectares). On June 4, 1790, Cornelius J. Bogert, a New York City attorney acting for the Dutch Reformed Church, announced that the entire Valentine property, including the new barn, orchard and the stone house, would be sold on July 5th at the Coffee House,[119] but once again there were no takers.

Valentine, in a last desperate attempt to retain something, on February 21, 1791, announced a public auction would be held on March 15th at his stone house where all, or sections of, his property would be offered for sale. Alternatively, he was willing to mortgage the land to anyone willing to lend him £1,000 by April 1st, frankly admitting that he was selling his land becuase he needed the money. Nothing seems to have come from his efforts either.

On January 17, 1792, the Church tried to sell the land once again, this time using Peter P. Van Zandt and John de Peyster of New York City as its agents. As opposed to previous attempts, there would be no public auction. Moreover, the land in Yonkers that Emmons had assigned to the Dutch Reformed Church to sell was not offered. Therefore, only 365 acres (146 hectares) were advertised. In addition to the stone house, the barn and the orchard, the location on the public highway was deemed an attraction, as was the fact that most of the land was already divided by good stone fences. The agents suggested such potential uses for the property as keeping a tavern, raising cattle and sheep, and growing grain. For flexibility, they were willing to sell all or part of the land, and promised that, if sold, Isaac Valentine, who still lived there, would vacate the premises by April 1st,[120] just in time for the spring planting season. However, no one came forward to purchase.

Therefore, Isaac Valentine had the opportunity to spend one more season on his farm and in the stone house he had built in 1758. Once again, he could try to eke out a living, attempting to raise the elusive cash he needed to pay his debts, and once again, he would fail.

In the fall of 1792, Valentine's property attracted a prospective purchaser. A resident of New York, Isaac Varian, made the necessary inquiries. In addition to the land in Fordham in the town of Westchester, the agents also called Varian's attention to the land in the town of Yonkers Emmons had assigned to the Church. Varian agreed to buy all but 5½ acres (just over 2 hectares) of the Fordham property and all of Valentine's Yonkers lands, a total of nearly 500 acres (almost 200 hectares). On November 26, 1792, Isaac Varian paid the Reformed Protestant Dutch Church in New York City £1,550 New York currency, and all that property, including the stone house, was placed in his possession.

Thus, at the end of 1792, after 34 years, Isaac Valentine left the farmlands that he had purchased from the Dutch Reformed Church and the stone house he had built and in which his children were born. He was destined to spend the last years of his life in White Plains.[121] His life and livelihood had been shattered by financial ruin brought on by the effects of the war. In a sense, he was as much a casualty of the American Revolution as the soldier who had fought in a battle and was seriously wounded. However, with new owners, the continued survival of the house could not be guaranteed.

CHAPTER SEVEN

Since 1793: Years of Preservation

Isaac Varian, the new proprietor of the stone house, was the youngest son of a butcher in New York City bearing the same name. Born in 1740, he also became a butcher, growing prosperous in the process. He had married Hannah Van Den Berg in 1765 and was the father of her six children, two of whom were twins. Tragically, half of these children died before reaching the age of two. Thus, by the end of 1775, he was left with Isaac, then his only son, and his daughters, Mary and Elizabeth. Moreover, in that same year, his wife died, and he became a widower. At the onset of the Revolution, Varian zealously supported the American side, and had fled British-held New York City for the safety of upper Westchester County. He also ardently wooed, and in 1777, married Alletta Harsen. By his second wife, he had four children. Unfortunately, the first two, patriotically named Catherine Washington and George Washington, died young, while Jacob Harsen and Richard managed to survive their wartime infancies. When Varian purchased Valentine's property, his 25-year old eldest son, a gardener in New York City, had just recently married Tamar Leggett of West Farms. Isaac's 23-year old daughter, Mary, had married Gilbert Coutant of New Rochelle in 1789. Since his new son-in-law had been a drover driving herds past the stone house, perhaps the butcher had first received favorable word about the Valentine property from him. Whatever the case, it was with his second wife, and 17-year old Elizabeth, 11-year old Jacob Harsen, and 9-year old Richard, that the 52-year old Isaac Varian took possession of the stone house and the farmland upon which it rested.[122]

It appears that Varian became wholly committed to his farm and to the town of Westchester. Despite his background as a butcher, he consistently identified himself as a farmer from that community. Faced with working the expanse of land that straddled the boundary line of the towns of Westchester and Yonkers, he utilized some of the same methods as had Isaac Valentine. Slaves helped him perform some tasks, and, in 1800, Varian owned three of them. In addition, it is likely that he hired some servants as well. In 1800, two young women and one girl under the age of ten were living in his house, and since no female members of his family were of those ages at the time, it is likely that they were servants.[123]

Just as Isaac Valentine had to mortgage part of his landholdings to obtain cash, Isaac Varian had to do so too. On February 25, 1801, the inhabitant of the stone house borrowed $1,403 in pieces of eight from Augustus Van Cortlandt using as collateral a 100 acre (400 hectare) dwelling tract in what was then Yonkers, formerly the property of William Betts. In addition, perhaps with a touch of irony, on April 30, 1803, Varian borrowed $325 from Isaac Valentine, Jr., and John Valentine, Jr., both of whom lived in New York City, pledging 25 acres (10 hectares) of the old Fordham Manor farm as security. Unlike his predecessor, however, Varian was able to repay his debts, the first in 1814 and the second in 1804.[124]

As Isaac Valentine had his blacksmith's skills to supplement his life as a farmer, so did Isaac Varian have other interests. In 1806, the town of Westchester advertised the availability of a lease for its mill on Westchester Creek. The town owned the mill, but the cost of adding new mill stones and the structure to house them had produced a debt of $5,153.02. The rent charged was designed to reduce and perhaps eliminate this debt. Varian stepped forward and leased the town's mill for 14 years at $550 a year. In addition, he advanced the Westchester Board of Trustees $35,000, for which he charged interest, while his annual rent would be invested by the town to produce the funds to pay the mill debt. Varian took possession of the mill on May 6, 1806. By 1815, the town was able to discharge the $35,000 loan Varian had advanced, while the mill debt had been nearly paid. Five years of the lease still remained to provide the town with a steady income.[125] Thus, Varian had become a major source of the funds Westchester needed, and, in the process, had become a miller, receiving a profit for every service he performed for the farmers who used his mill.

Isaac Varian also raised cash by selling some of his land. For instance, on December 14, 1801, he sold for $550 six acres (almost 2½ hectares) of salt meadow in what was then Yonkers near the Albany Post Road. Alexander McComb, whose farm adjoined that property, was the buyer. Similarly, Varian sold about 10 acres (4 hectares) in Yonkers to Samuel Briggs for $500 on April 25, 1807.[126]

However, unlike Isaac Valentine, Varian appears to have been a financial success, and he was even in a position to lend money. On March 29, 1814, David Ferris and his wife, Ann, borrowed what was then a substantial sum from the town's miller. To secure the loan, they pledged as collateral four tracts of land in Throg's Neck totalling 330 acres (132 hectares). When the amount was repaid in 1819 with interest, Isaac Varian received $3,520.[127]

Life in the stone house centered around the joys and sorrows of the Varian family. Undoubtedly, on occasion, his eldest son, Isaac, came from New York City to visit. At those times, the son probably proudly showed off his own son, Isaac Leggett. This grandson would eventually become the most prominent family member. However, it is probable that the old man's daughter, Mary, also journeyed to the farm from New York City, bringing her husband, Gilbert Coutant, who had once been a drover, but who had now established himself as a grocer. Certainly, the old man had affection for his son-in-law and also valued his judgment.

Sorrow came to the stone house on July 30, 1801, when Alletta, Isaac Varian's second wife, died after 24 years of marriage, nine of them on the farm. Joy followed in 1803 when Elizabeth, the youngest daughter of his first wife, married Samuel Briggs, to whom the old man would sell some of his land in Yonkers in 1807.

In 1803, a lonely 63-year old Isaac Varian married for a third time. His new bride was Jane Betts, a young woman many years his junior. She was brought into the stone house, sharing it not only with her husband, but with two grown sons by her husband's second wife—22-year old Jacob Harsen and 20-year old Richard—both of whom were close to her age.

Despite their difference in age, life for the old man and his young bride was happy at first. Children came in rapid succession, all of whom were born in the stone house. A daughter, Dorcas, was born in 1804, followed by another daughter, Jane, the next year. Their first son together arrived in 1807 and was honored with the name of Isaac Varian's son-in-law, Gilbert Coutant. Another son, Michael, who was to play an important role in preserving his birthplace, was born November 26, 1808. Twins, James and Hannah, were delivered almost one year later when the old man was 69.

By that time, Jacob Harsen and Richard had married and had begun lives of their own. Jacob had wed Hannah Leggett of West Farms in 1806, while Richard had married Elizabeth Fowler in 1810.[128] Their father gave them a start in life by selling them jointly a neighboring farm in Yonkers of just over 17 acres (almost 7 hectares) for $1,340 on the same day Samuel Briggs had purchased his land.[129]

The year 1809 in a sense marked a watershed in Isaac Varian's life. Although he continued to gain financially with his farming, milling and real estate ventures, his personal life began to be marked by almost unrelieved tragedy. On January 30th of that year, his daughter, Mrs. Elizabeth Briggs, died after only six years of marriage, not reaching her 37th birthday. About this time, his young wife, Jane, began to lose her mind. It is not certain what was the cause of her descent into insanity.

On top of that, the aging Isaac Varian developed dropsy in the chest. As the cavity that held his lungs filled with fluid, it became more difficult for him to breathe. Finally, on March 29, 1820, the old man succumbed to the disease, dying three months short of his 80th birthday.[130]

The estate was administered by Isaac, the old man's eldest son by his first wife, Jacob Harsen, the eldest son by his second wife, and by his trusted son-in-law, Gilbert Coutant. However, several factors complicated matters. The young widow, Jane, inherited all his lands for the rest of her life. Unfortunately, she was legally insane. Moreover, all of the old man's children who had survived into adulthood also inherited equal shares of the farm in their own right as tenants in common. These included Jane's children, all of them under the age of 17 and, thus, legally minors. In addition, Mary, Isaac and Elizabeth Briggs, three of the old man's grandchildren by his predeceased daughter, Elizabeth, each held one-third of a share in the property, and they, too, were minors. Therefore, a great portion of Isaac Varian's heirs were legally incompetent to make decisions regarding their legacy.

Consequently, Isaac Varian, the gardener, and Gilbert Coutant, the grocer, both living in New York and both of whom were administrators of the estate, brought separate bills of complaint to the Court of Chancery on August 4, 1820. On October 31st, the court appointed Jacobus Dyckman of New York City and Andrew Corsa and James Varian (a cousin of the heirs) both of Westchester, as commissioners to divide the property, and four days later, decreed that it be sold to the highest bidders at a public auction. The fate of the stone house once again was jeopardized.

The public auction of the property took place in the town of Westchester at the stone farmhouse by the side of the Boston Post Road on April 18, 1821. James Bathgate took just over 76 acres (almost 3½ hectares) at the western end of the old Fordham Manor farm bidding $2,671.15 for it. Benjamin Lent of Eastchester obtained land straddling the Westchester–Yonkers border, part of which had once belonged to Richard Montgomery, for $659.06. Two lots in Westchester and one in Yonkers totalling just over 166 acres (about 66½ hectares) went to Isaac Corsa for $2,087. However, two parts of the old farm were purchased by members of the Varian family. Jacob Harsen, who lived in Yonkers, purchased the remainder of the Montgomery farm, a salt meadow on Spuyten Duyvil Creek and another near Tippet's Neck, a total of about 35 acres (14 hectares), for $1,001.10. Richard Varian, the youngest son by the old man's second wife, purchased the farm upon which the stone house stood for $4,104. Thus, the sale of Isaac Varian's vast farmland produced a total of $10,522.31. After the sum realized on the sale was divided among the heirs, two trust funds were established, one for the minors, and one for the demented Jane Varian to last her lifetime. The able Gilbert Coutant became both the guardian of the children and the administrator of Jane Varian's trust fund.

In the meantime, Richard Varian occupied the stone house that was built by Isaac Valentine in 1758. However, his farm was only a fraction of its original size. The main portion of the property consisted only of slightly more than 61 acres (about 24½ hectares) north of the Boston Post Road roughly between today's Jerome and Tryon Avenues south of the border that then existed between the towns of Westchester and Yonkers. The house rested on this land. The remainder of the farm consisted of just over 7 acres (almost 3 hectares) across the road from the house upon which the barn stood.[131] Perhaps it was the same barn erected by Isaac Valentine in 1789.

This farm that Richard Varian now hoped to work was greatly changed from the one his father had purchased in 1792. In addition to the vast reduction in size, the road which passed through it in front of the stone house had lost a great deal of its previous importance. The construction of the Harlem Bridge (on the site of today's Third Avenue Bridge) and the approach road to it provided travelers from New England with a shorter and more direct route to New York City than the road to the King's Bridge. Throughout his father's tenure, more people began using the new thoroughfare (today's Boston Road) and fewer strangers passed by the stone house each year. Those who did use the old route were neighbors.

There was also a change in farm labor. Since 1799, a state law had provided for gradual emancipation of slaves, and in 1818, a law had passed decreeing the abolition of slavery on July 4, 1827. However, by 1812, most slaves in the town of Westchester, indeed, in the entire state, had been freed. Therefore, Richard Varian had to work his farm himself, along with his children, and, perhaps, a hired hand or two.

Moreover, the growth of the United States had an important effect on farming in the vicinity of Richard Varian's stone house. The migration of people into the fertile Great Plains opened up vast fields producing huge amounts of wheat, corn, and other grain, which had been staples of the farmers of the east. The opening of the Erie Canal in 1825 tapped this immense supply, flooding the markets of New York City. Varian and the other farmers in his neighborhood were forced to change to survive.

It is likely that Richard Varian could not cope with these rapid changes. One year after he took possession of the farm, he approached Gilbert Coutant to borrow money from the two trust funds. He borrowed $1,946.04 from the Jane Varian trust, promising to pay $58.58 a year in semi-annual payments as long as the insane woman lived. Another $2,510.48 was borrowed from the trust fund for the minors at a yearly interest rate of 6%. Both loans were secured by the Varian farm.[132] Unfortunately, Richard Varian ultimately defaulted on both loans.

In 1829, Gilbert Coutant, on behalf of both trusts, sued the owner of the stone house at the Court of Chancery in Albany to recover the principal and interest that was due. On September 2nd, the court ordered that the Varian farm once again be sold at public auction, and Aaron Ward, a Master in Chancery in Westchester, seized it for sale. For the second time in one decade, the existence of the stone house was placed in jeopardy.

It was at this moment the first in a series of remarkable men, whose attitudes and actions were chiefly responsible for preserving the house for posterity, stepped forward. This was Michael Varian, fourth child of Isaac and his third wife. Born and raised in the stone house, he was forced to leave it at the age of 12 after his father died. Brought to New York City, he worked with his brother-in-law and guardian, Gilbert Coutant, in the grocery business. However, he never forgot his birthplace, and by the end of the decade, a combination of circumstances existed which enabled him to obtain it. He had recently married Martha Huestis, thus starting a family of his own. His guardian had also just left the grocery business to become a lumber merchant, which, of course, would force Michael Varian to make a decision about the way he intended to earn a living. At the same time, Richard Varian's farm was offered for sale.

Consequently, when Aaron Ward held the auction at the stone house on November 27, 1829, Michael Varian, one day after he reached his 21st birthday, bid $3,600 for the farm, and won it. To help finance the transaction, he borrowed $2,200 from the Jane Varian trust at 6% interest, using the land as collateral.[133] The remainder probably came from the money he had just inherited from the trust fund for the minor children, since he had just reached the age of majority. Once he moved back to his birthplace, he would not leave it for 63½ years.

Because of the changed economic circumstances, Michael Varian knew he could not raise grain on his farm profitably. Therefore, both he and his neighbors, indeed almost all the farmers of Westchester County, stopped producing wheat and began supplying a growing New York City with fresh vegetables, butter, poultry, eggs, lambs, and calves.[134]

To operate his farm, Michael Varian, like most farmers, constantly needed money, and in 1832, he once again borrowed from the Jane Varian trust fund, taking $1,000 at 6% interest, using his land as security a second time. Four years later, his elder sister, Jane, lent him another $1,000 at 6% interest, and the farm was pledged as collateral this time as well.[135]

These debts had remained outstanding for over two decades when the country experienced the depression of 1857. It is probably because of the effect of this sharp downturn in the economy that Michael Varian had to borrow once more, and again, the only thing he had to use for collateral was his land. Thus, on December 19, 1859, he took out two loans from the Yonkers Savings Bank, one for $1,000 and the other for $5,000. On the same day, he turned to his older sister for a second time and borrowed an additional $3,000, but only the 61 acres (24½ hectares) north of the road was used as security for this loan.[136]

It was in 1860 that a crisis stage was reached. Although

Michael Varian was able to repay the one debt he had owed to his sister since 1836, his mother, after suffering decades in insanity, finally passed away. While this would ultimately result in the proprietor of the stone house receiving his share as an heir in the dissolved trust fund, it also meant that all loans and investments made in the name of the fund first would have to be collected, and he owed that fund a substantial sum. Gilbert Coutant had died in 1846, and the administration of the Jane Varian trust had been exercised by two others in succession until James Acker of Greenburgh, the last administrator, obtained an order from the State Supreme Court in White Plains on July 9, 1860, turning over collection of the outstanding debts to the Westchester County Treasurer.[137]

Michael Varian was unable to repay his debts immediately. Indeed, he had to borrow more. On December 8, 1866, his sister Jane advanced him funds once again, this time $4,000 at 6% interest on the small barn lot. The same day, Daniel Mapes lent him $12,000 at 7% interest on the rest of the farm.[138] Using these funds, he was able to discharge the debts previously owed to the Jane Varian trust, the Yonkers Savings Bank, and his sister.[139] Because of returning prosperity, aided by the sale on September 6, 1869, of all 13 acres (5.2 hectares) of his farm west of today's Mosholu Parkway, Varian was able to eliminate his debt to Daniel Mapes in the fall of 1869, and by 1875, the last obligation to his sister was discharged.[140] For the rest of his life, Michael Varian's farm would be free from debt.

While displaying the agility to retain possession of the stone house that was his birthplace, Michael Varian played a more subtle, but, perhaps, more important role in preserving the structure. He always considered his family an important part of his life, and his family responded with love and trust. When he first obtained the farm in 1829 because of Richard Varian's financial troubles, he had no obligation to his half brother at all. Yet, he took in Richard's son, Alfred, to help in the farm work, and the lad remained until he reached the age of 19 in 1833, when he left to be apprenticed to a butcher in New York City. Years later, Alfred would look back fondly at his work on his Uncle Michael's farm.[141] Similarly, in 1832, when his youngest brother, James, who had recently passed his 22nd birthday, needed cash immediately, Michael gave him $1,070, despite his own financial straits at the time, in return for his brother's share in the Jane Varian trust fund.[142]

Michael Varian had fewer direct dealings with Isaac Leggett Varian, his father's grandson, the son of Michael's eldest half brother, Isaac. However, he must have been proud of his nephew's political career as an ardent Jacksonian Democrat, which over the span of a decade moved him from the state Assembly to New York City's Board of Aldermen, to the presidency of that body, to, finally, election as mayor of the city in 1839.[143]

However, by that time, Michael Varian was more interested in his immediate family, which was growing. Five children were born in the stone house—Martha, Michael, Jesse Huestis, Isaac and Jane. Unfortunately, Jane died in infancy,[144] but the rest were reared in the house, helping on the farm. Even after they had grown up and married, the children never moved far away, and they frequently visited their parents. In fact, they became so attached to their parents that five of the eight grandchildren were born in the old farmhouse.[145]

The bond of love and trust that Michael Varian forged over the 63½ years of his ownership of the farm spilled over, perhaps unwittingly, to attachment to the house in which he lived. When he first occupied the stone structure, it was just another farmhouse. Through the decades, the birth of children and grandchildren provided a bond of sentiment between those members of Michael's family and the structure. In addition, the constant visits back home year after year as Michael Varian grew ever older made the house a central part in the lives of each family member, with the aging man taking the role of patriarch and the house as his seat. When the century had reached the three-quarter mark, few people could remember when Michael Varian did not live there, and practically no one could recall if any other family had occupied it. By that time, the old stone structure was no longer another farmhouse, but it was the Varian Homestead, with a character and meaning of its own. It was a source of stability in a changing world.

The construction in the early 1840s of the New York and Harlem Railroad from Manhattan Island paralleling the west side of the Bronx River valley had profoundly affected Michael Varian's world in two ways. First, with the establishment of a

Isaac Leggett Varian, Mayor of New York, 1839–1841. By W.J. Morgan & Company. *Courtesy of The New-York Historical Society.*

station at the western end of Williams's Bridge, the people of the neighborhood who wished to journey to New York City could use the faster railroad rather than the slower land route over the road past the stone farmhouse. What little steady traffic that had continued using the old highway disappeared altogether, and it became merely a lane connecting the two small villages of Kingsbridge and Williamsbridge. By the 1850s, no one even called it the Boston Post Road anymore.[146]

The second consequence of the railroad's construction was more substantial. Large numbers of people rode the rails out of the overcrowded city to re-establish themselves in the country atmosphere of lower Westchester County. The population of the half of the town of Westchester west of the Bronx River grew so rapidly that in 1846 it was erected into a separate town of West Farms, and Michael Varian's stone house was near the northernmost edge of the new town.

As the years passed, the influence of the burgeoning metropolis on Manhattan Island began to manifest itself in ever more direct ways. After the Civil War, that part of Isaac Varian's old farm that had been purchased by James Bathgate was turned into the Jerome Park Racetrack for the amusement of the city gentry. In addition, land just north of Michael Varian's farm was sold to become Woodlawn Cemetery, designed to serve primarily as the final resting place for well-to-do New Yorkers. Finally, in 1874, New York City annexed the town of West Farms, and the Varian Homestead was now within the bounds of the metropolis.

Through it all, Michael Varian remained on his farm, working it to the best of his ability, and making his house a focal point for his family. A major blow was the death of his wife, Martha, in 1876,[147] but the aging man kept on operating his farmland until he retired in 1885 at the age of 77. Even then, he continued living in the Varian Homestead, but daily operation of the farm was assumed by his 47-year old son, Jesse Huestis.[148]

A few years later, New York City took a piece of the Varian farm to build a reservoir for distribution to the annexed district of waters of the upper Bronx River impounded by the Kensico Dam. This new structure was built immediately east

SINCE 1793: YEARS OF PRESERVATION

of the Varian Homestead, athwart the old road that passed in front of the house. To facilitate traffic, a driveway (today's Reservoir Oval) was constructed around the new basin. On December 4, 1888, water was admitted to the Williamsbridge Reservoir for the first time.[149]

The Valentine-Varian House in 1874 or 1875. This is the oldest known photograph of the structure. Standing in front of the picket fence is Jesse Huestis Varian. Seated next to him is his wife, Lorinda Conklin Varian. The patriarch of the family, Michael Varian, son of Isaac Varian, is seated to the right. *The Bronx County Historical Society Collection.*

In April, 1893, in the 84th year of his life, Michael Varian died in the old stone house he had helped to preserve.[150] The house and the farm were inherited by all of his children equally, but only Jesse Huestis Varian and his wife, Lorinda Conklin, lived at the Homestead, and it was they who were chiefly responsible for its upkeep.

Unfortunately, old Michael's death coincided with the onset of a deep depression which hit farmers across the nation particularly hard. At first, Jesse Huestis Varian attempted to cope with the downturn in prices by concentrating only on milk production and distribution.[151] Matters did not improve, and by 1896, Jesse and his brother, Isaac, who was then a widower, began to share in the operation of the farm.[152] It was obvious the farm was not bringing in enough cash to support all those living in the Varian Homestead, and Jesse made the decision to move to Mount Vernon, leaving his brother in possession. To obtain the necessary funds to keep the operation going, on December 29, 1897, Michael, Jesse Huestis and Isaac Varian, along with their sister, Martha Varian Archer, all the childen of old Michael, borrowed $50,000 at 5% interest from the Union Dime Savings Bank, using the farm as collateral.[153]

By that time, the economy began to recover, but the advances which occurred were not necessarily advantageous for the farm. In 1898, the borough of The Bronx was created and this, along with the continuing migration of population from Manhattan, caused several rapid changes. The Jerome Park Racetrack had been closed and a new, larger, reservoir was under construction there. Much of the old farmland surrounding the Varian Homestead had been divided into lots for sale as sites for single family frame houses. A number of houses already had been erected. Mosholu Parkway was constructed along the western edge of the Varian farm and plans were made to cut several streets through the property. It became increasingly difficult to operate a farm under such circumstances. With a need to pay off the debt to the bank and facing the prospect of increased tax assessments for the new streets, accompanied by the increased value of the land itself, it seemed prudent to sell the farm.

Accordingly, Isaac Varian moved out of his family's homestead, re-establishing himself in Stamford, Connecticut. Surveyors divided the farm into home lots, finishing their work on April 22, 1905, and filing their map on October 6th. On June 2nd, the heirs of Michael Varian sold the entire farm for $260,000 to Alfred E. Hanson of Brooklyn, helping finance the sale with two loans to him, one for $17,000 and the other for $12,000, both at 4½% interest.

Yet Michael's children still valued the house in which they

SINCE 1793: YEARS OF PRESERVATION

The Valentine-Varian House in 1899. Van Cortlandt Avenue East is still a country road. *The Bronx County Historical Society Collection.*

were born. As long as they held an interest in it by the possibility of Hanson defaulting on the loans, they were going to make sure that the Varian Homestead would not be destroyed. They placed in the document extending Hanson the loans not only the usual warning that the entire principal would become due within 30 days in case the interest or taxes were not paid, but that the family could demand complete payment of the principal "immediately upon the actual or threatened demolition of any building on said premises."[154]

The Varian family applied the proceeds of the sale to retiring the 1897 debt to the Union Dime Savings Bank, while Hanson, on the same day he purchased the property, sold the entire farm to the Mosholu Parkway Realty Company for subsequent resale as home lots. The funds he ultimately received he used to repay his two loans to the Varians.[155] Thus, before the month of October, 1905, was out, all restrictions as to the demolition of the stone house were eliminated, and once again its existence was in jeopardy.

The Varian farm was sold at auction, and the block upon which the stone house rested was purchased on October 23, 1905, for $4,000 by William Frank Beller. The transaction was largely financed by a loan of $3,900 from the Mosholu Parkway Realty Company at 5% interest, which Beller was able to repay in two years. The deed contained a restrictive covenant designed to keep the neighborhood a largely residential one of single family homes, at least until May 1, 1915. It is ironic that this covenant prohibited the erection of a smith's forge or a slaughterhouse on the property[156] when the man who had built the house in 1758 was a blacksmith and the man who had purchased it in 1792 was a butcher.

William F. Beller was the second extraordinary man whose attitude and actions led to the preservation of the old stone house. He, and those who followed him in preserving the structure, were remarkable for what they did considering the age in which they did it. The twentieth century was ushered in as an age of progress, when everything new and innovative was valued and almost anything old was considered obsolete. It was the future to which people looked with confidence. In

SINCE 1793: YEARS OF PRESERVATION

The Valentine-Varian House in 1905. The rise to the right is the wall of the Williamsbridge Reservoir. *The Bronx County Historical Society Collection.*

such a culture, anyone taking steps to preserve an old house, especially if he owned it, was rare. Beller, an expert on duty and export-import law, was in charge of a large department in the United States Customs House. Although he lived in Manhattan, he realized that the ancient dwelling was important historically and should be preserved, and he had purchased it with this idea in mind.[157]

When Beller purchased the house, the old road in front of it was being widened and named Van Cortlandt Avenue East, while Woodlawn Road (today's Bainbridge Avenue) was under construction between the farmhouse and the reservoir. Since he lived in Manhattan, he arranged to have an elderly gentleman stay in the house rent free to see that nothing was destroyed. This man occupied his time making violins.[158]

About 1910, the new owner was faced with making a major renovation of the old house. It was at this time that most of the cellar windows were added, the dilapidated porch was torn down and replaced with a replica of the original design, and a new door and sidelights were affixed. Modern living also required the installation of a steam heating system and plumbing for an indoor bathroom. The fireplaces inside the house were bricked up because of the new methods of heating.[159]

By the 1920s, the west wing, probably the oldest part of the house, which had been converted into a kitchen, was judged structurally unsafe. Sadly, William F. Beller had the entire wing demolished, burying the stones which had formed the facade on the site.[160]

The Valentine-Varian House soon after the west wing had been destroyed. Bainbridge Avenue to the front is a dirt road. *The Bronx County Historical Society collection.*

Meanwhile, the neighborhood had undergone a radical change. The extension of the Third Avenue El up Webster Avenue and of the Lexington Avenue subway via an elevated portion along Jerome Avenue induced thousands of people to move into the area. Apartment houses, one of which was erected behind the stone house, were built to accommodate the newcomers, and shops were provided for them along nearby Bainbridge Avenue.

During these years, the house began to receive increasing attention from local and architectural historians. Soon after the last Varian had left, Randall Comfort noted the structure's background in his *History of Bronx Borough*. In 1912, Stephen Jenkins included it among the places he deemed worthy of preservation when he wrote *The Story of The Bronx*. In 1926, Otto Hufeland, in his *Westchester County during the American Revolution*, became the first to call the historic structure the Valentine-Varian House. James L. Wells, Louis F. Haffen, and Josiah A. Briggs called it a landmark in their 1927 *The Bronx and Its People: A History*. In 1934, the Historic American Buildings Survey of the United States Department of the Interior included the old stone house among those it investigated. New York architect James Gambaro took field notes for the survey, and a series of blueprints was made.[161]

The Valentine-Varian House in April, 1934. The apartment houses behind the colonial edifice hem in the old house and illustrate the rapid march of urbanization in the neighborhood. *The Bronx County Historical Society Collection.*

William F. Beller died in 1936, leaving the Valentine-Varian House to his son, William Charles Beller. An electrical engineer, the son was also fluent in many languages and had a wide range of interests, including literature, natural history, botany, electronics, and history. His father had impressed him with the house's historical importance, and he was determined to carry out the intention to preserve the structure.[162] Because of this, William C. Beller became the third remarkable man whose actions and attitudes were instrumental in preserving the old stone house.

William C. Beller hired architect M.W. Del Gaudio to plan the reconstruction of the demolished west wing with the intention of putting it to a modern use as a one car garage. The plans were completed on July 26, 1936, and the garage was subsequently erected.[163]

Beller, like his father, resided in Manhattan. Therefore, when the elderly violin maker retired, a man who was in the construction business offered to live in the Valentine-Varian House and make what repairs were necessary at Beller's expense. He took a bit of the porch off, mended some of the window sills, and added a bathroom.[164]

Through these years, the neighborhood continued to grow, especially with the construction of the Sixth Avenue subway, with its last stop nearby at Bainbridge Avenue and East 206th Street. The increased population of the area was a factor which led in 1936 to the draining of the reservoir just east of the old stone house and its reconstruction into Williamsbridge Oval Park.

Sometime after 1956, a second wing was added to the Valentine-Varian House on its east end, but the severe housing shortage in New York City coupled with William C. Beller's determination to preserve the old farmhouse were more important factors in determining its future. Since the early 1940s, the Daughters of the American Revolution had shown an interest in perpetuating the structure through its committees and in its correspondence with Beller, and by 1959, they appeared to be the logical group to take care of it. At the same time, Alexander and Daniel Cole, two brothers in the real estate business

SINCE 1793: YEARS OF PRESERVATION

The Valentine-Varian House in 1956. A neat, white picket fence separates the lawn from a paved Van Cortlandt Avenue East. The house has a suburban air, despite the apartment houses behind it. The garage, erected in 1936, is to the left of the main structure. *The Bronx County Historical Society Collection.*

with an office nearby on Mosholu Parkway, became interested in the property as a site to build an apartment house. Bronx Borough President James J. Lyons, meanwhile, offered his cooperation in relocating the structure onto city land.[165]

Therefore, on November 11, 1959, William C. Beller signed an agreement with the Cole brothers for the sale of the land with an understanding that the old stone house would be preserved and moved off the site within 60 days. Beller was to obtain within 30 days a commitment from the DAR to maintain the building, together with a financial indemnification to the city for the house's cost and expense. However, if such an undertaking were not received, this clause was to be considered null and void. The agreed purchase price for the site was $85,000, with Beller receiving $8,500 immediately.[166]

News of this transaction reached Bert Gumpert, a columnist for the Bronx edition of the *New York Post*. Gumpert was also a founder of the four-year old Bronx County Historical Society, and he alerted the Society's officers as to what was happening. Acting on their direction, he contacted the DAR and the borough president's office thinking it would be desirable for the Society to use the rooms in the house as an exhibit space.[167]

Beller, meanwhile, was finding difficulty obtaining the necessary commitment from the DAR, which the organization eventually found financially impossible to give. On December 21st, the attorney for the Cole brothers dispatched a note to Beller's attorney, Nathan Kestnbaum, invoking the provision declaring the preservation clause in the agreement null and void as of December 28th, making the notice official in a letter of January 14, 1960.[168]

By this time, The Bronx County Historical Society was showing increasing interest in the Valentine-Varian House. The DAR had written to the Society, and on February 3, 1960, Bert Gumpert and Dr. Theodore Kazimiroff volunteered to contact the city's Parks Department about the relocation of the building.[169] Kazimiroff, a dentist by profession, had a wide range of interests in the sciences, arts, and humanities, including an absorbing interest in local history. Along with Bert Gumpert, he had founded The Bronx County Historical Society, and had served as its first president. He was also the official Bronx Borough Historian, and he was the fourth remarkable man whose actions and attitudes led to the preservation of the stone house.

The following month, the Parks Department told the Society that the city had no money to finance the moving of the house to a proposed new site, and at the Society's behest, the department estimated the total cost of removal, excavation of a new foundation, installation of utilities, building restoration and site improvement to be $88,200, and demanded a bond of $95,000 from William C. Beller to do the job. That was $10,000 more than the sales price for the property upon which the house stood. Beller was aghast. He had expected the sum to be closer to $20,000.[170]

Nevertheless, on April 2, 1960, Beller's attorney, Nathan Kestnbaum, appeared before a meeting of The Bronx County Historical Society, expressing his client's wish to donate the Valentine-Varian House to the Society, assuming all cost of its removal and restoration, and setting up a small trust fund for its maintenance. A committee was then formed, upon which Theodore Kazimiroff took the lead, to act on the Society's behalf.[171]

However, as events were to prove, the ensuing five years were to see the old stone house placed in the greatest danger of destruction since the harrowing days of the American Revolution. The Parks Department insisted that the premises be vacated before it would even consider the question of moving the house to a new site. Therefore, the last tenant in the building had to leave,[172] and the old fieldstone farmhouse was uninhabited for the first time since it was built 202 years earlier. No one then expected it would take five years for the goal of moving the building to be reached.

Meanwhile, William C. Beller continually postponed closing the sale of the property, while the Cole brothers believed the original agreement to be in force without the preservation clause. Finally, on May 3, 1960, a summons was issued at the request of the Cole brothers calling on Beller to appear in State Supreme Court in Bronx County to compel him to complete the terms of the agreement they had all signed.[173] Beller countered by contending that his sole desire, as understood by all, was to preserve the historic house, and that the sum of $95,000 required by the Parks Department made the performance of the contract impossible. He offered to return the $8,500 paid to him and asked that the complaint be dismissed.[174] On August 3rd, Justice Charles A. Loreto decreed that, although by the literal terms of the agreement, Beller had defaulted, the unanticipated costs and the lack of full trial to examine the historic importance of the house made a summary order to carry out the agreement's terms inequitable. Therefore, the Cole brother's request for such an order was denied.[175]

The Cole brothers immediately filed an appeal.[176] However, on November 16th, the parties came to an agreement out of court. It was agreed that both sides would try to procure the permission of city agencies to move the building to a new site across Bainbridge Avenue between Van Cortlandt Avenue East and East 208th Street. In addition, William C. Beller agreed to pay the first $65,000 for the cost of moving the house, while the Cole brothers would pay up to $10,000 if any additional monies were required, and Beller up to $10,000 beyond that, if needed.[177]

William Charles Beller about 1961. *The Bronx County Historical Society Collection.*

However, obtaining the approval of several New York City departments, commissions, boards and agencies took longer than anticipated. By May 24, 1964, the appropriate bodies had made the removal of the old stone house possible, and William C. Beller and the Cole brothers modified and amplified their agreement. Beller agreed to pay up to $80,000 to relocate the structure plus $1,000 in architect's fees. In addition, it was recognized that further approval for specific items, such as map changes and plans, had yet to be achieved.[178]

While such approvals were being sought, the Valentine-

Varian House remained boarded up and empty, thus becoming a target for vandalism. Theodore Kazimiroff, acting on behalf of The Bronx County Historical Society, was ever vigilant in trying to protect the property.[179] He alerted residents of the neighborhood and the local police to watch for any untoward happenings, often patrolling outside the house himself. He mounted a strong campaign to inform the public about the historic importance of the old stone house, about its future as the Society's museum, and about the progress of the vandalism that happened there despite all efforts to prevent it.

By August, 1963, the *New York Times* noted that:

> shutters have been torn off, windows smashed, original doors ripped from hinges and holes big enough for an adult to pass through have been torn in the walls. . . . Copies of early American chandeliers have been smashed and the remaining fixtures have been ripped out of the low ceilings. Bottles filled with soft drinks that have been smashed against the walls have left huge stains that look like the work of an abstract artist.

At the same time, Kazimiroff warned, "An act of vandalism in the form of a fire or equally disastrous dawdling on the part of city officials will lead to the destruction forever of one of the few priceless remaining relics of Bronx antiquity."[180] On January 19, 1964, he added, "Vandalism and civic indifference are causing more havoc to this fine fieldstone house than all the assaults by both sides in the Revolution."[181] He kept repeating his warnings even as the city was slowly clearing the way for removal of the structure to its intended site.[182]

Finally, on May 4, 1965, sufficient progress toward reaching the goal of removing and preserving the Valentine-Varian House had been made, and William C. Beller officially sold the property to Mount Vernon Estates, Inc.,[183] a corporation run by the Cole brothers. The ensuing weeks were devoted to preparing the old stone house for removal from the site it had occupied for 207 years, a job performed by Nicholas Brothers of Yonkers, specialists in the field, following the plans of architect Anthony Signorelli. First, the two non-historic wings were demolished. Then, the 600 ton (more than 544 metric ton) dwelling, ribbed with steel bands and supported by steel beams, was tugged away from its old location at the northwest corner of Van Cortlandt Avenue East and Bainbridge Avenue, and drawn across the street by an enormous dolly on 48 wheels. On June 30th, it had made its way across Bainbridge Avenue and was parked for the night near the entrance to Williamsbridge Oval Park. On July 1, 1965, it was eased onto its new foundation with its front doorway for the first time facing westward. A delighted William C. Beller was there to take motion pictures of the event, and an equally delighted Theodore Kazimiroff was on hand to witness it. There, these two remarkable men met for the first time.[184]

The Valentine-Varian House in 1963. Three years of unoccupied existence gives evidence of neglect and vandalism. A hole has opened through the shingled roof, the eaves are torn, and weeds grow on a littered lawn. The two new wings to the right and left of the larger house also can be seen. *The Bronx County Historical Society Collection.*

SINCE 1793: YEARS OF PRESERVATION

The side and rear of the Valentine-Varian House. Vandals had climbed to the roof the the newest (east) wing and had torn the boards off the window to gain entrance to the structure. *The Bronx County Historical Society Collection.*

Nevertheless, much work still had to be done. As the new apartment house was rising on the original site, the old stone house had to be restored and the damage done by years of vandalism erased. Once that enormous task was completed, a caretaker had to be found. After that, an exhibit had to be mounted in the rooms reserved for museum use. Once again, Theodore Kazimiroff, acting for The Bronx County Historical Society, took a keen interest in the restoration. Significantly, on June 21, 1966, the Society's Board of Trustees was able to meet in the Valentine-Varian House for the first time.[185] The Board returned on November 15th to meet with Nathan Kestnbaum, William C. Beller's attorney, to be presented with the deed to the house and Beller's contribution toward its maintenance.[186]

Meanwhile, Theodore Kazimiroff worked to put the house in order and to mount the first exhibit for the opening of the museum. The task took a year and a half. At last, on Memorial Day, 1968, The Bronx County Historical Society opened the Valentine-Varian House to the public for the first time with an

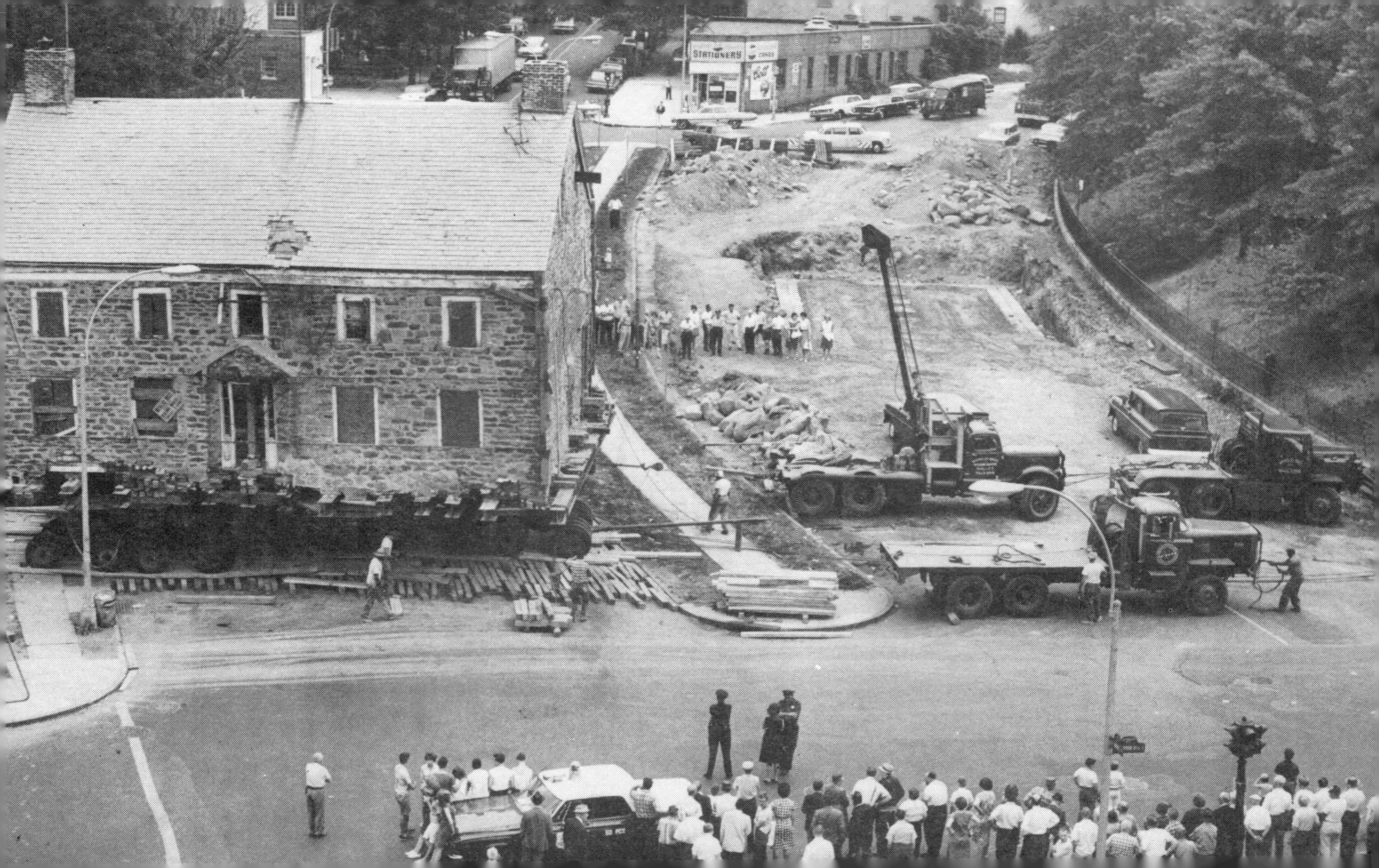
STATIONERY

Facing page: Moving the Valentine-Varian House across Bainbridge Avenue in 1965. The two wings and the porch were removed to facilitate the move. Among the spectators were William Charles Beller and Dr. Theodore Kazimiroff, who both worked for the relocation of the house. *The Bronx County Historical Society Collection.*

appropriate ribbon cutting ceremony. William C. Beller proudly signed the guest book as the first visitor.[187]

In part because of the controversy over the successful attempt to preserve the stone house, interest in the history of the structure had been aroused. In addition, The Bronx County Historical Society wanted to utilize every means it knew to insure that the Valentine-Varian House would never be demolished. Because of this, the New York City Landmarks Preservation Commission investigated the structure and found it had important architectural and historic merit illustrating the development and heritage of the city.[188] Similarly, the Society brought the house to the attention of state and federal authorities, and, as a result, in 1978, it was placed on the National Register of Historic Places.[189]

Dr. Theodore Kazimiroff speaks at the flagpole dedication ceremony, 1966. Seated to the right is Congressman Jonathan Bingham. *The Bronx County Historical Society Collection.*

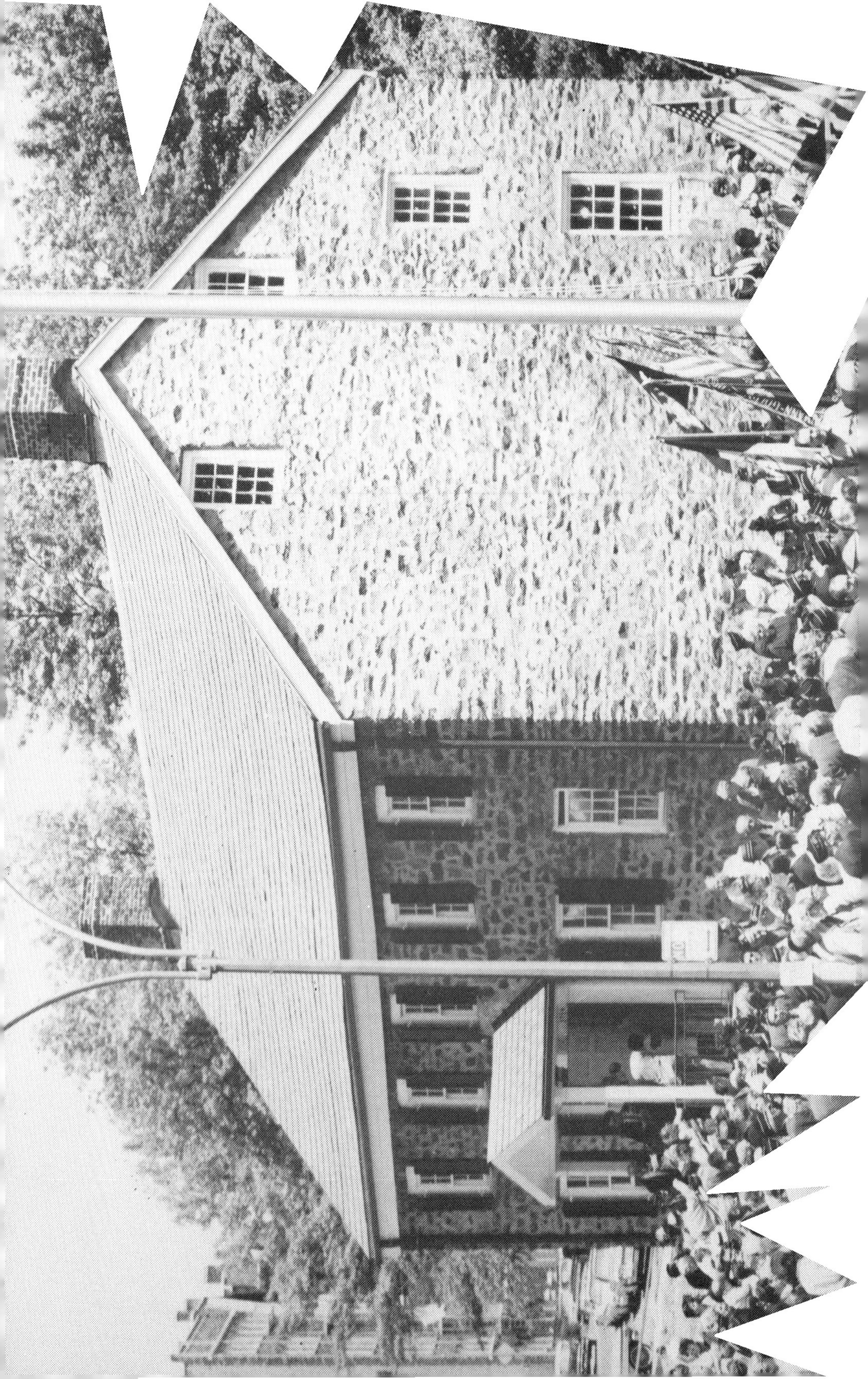

SINCE 1793: YEARS OF PRESERVATION

Facing page: The Valentine-Varian House two years before its opening as the Museum of Bronx History. On Memorial Day, 1966, the Neumann-Goldman Post of the Jewish War Veterans dedicated the memorial flagpole to the south of the new site of the house. *The Bronx County Historical Society Collection.*

Because of the efforts of Isaac Valentine, who tried to save his house from harm while living in a war zone; Michael Varian, who gave the house a character and meaning; William F. Beller; William C. Beller; and Theodore Kazimiroff, who all aided in preserving it, the Valentine-Varian House stands today. The Bronx County Historical Society is carrying on that tradition. Therefore, the old stone house will continue to exist as a legacy of the Revolution, reminding all persons of the events and suffering connected with the founding of the nation, and acting as a yardstick by which people can measure the growth and development of the surrounding neighborhood, The Bronx, and New York City.

Students from St. Pius High School examining exhibits in the Valentine-Varian House, May, 1976.

APPENDIX

The Architecture of the Valentine-Varian House

Although the Valentine–Varian House could not be considered outstanding in terms of being an architectural monument, it is an excellent example of a typical structure built in its time and place. There were no professional architects in colonial America when the house was built, and its design most likely came from the mind of Isaac Valentine, who, as a blacksmith, was a craftsman. Such craftsman-designed buildings are called "vernacular" by architectural historians, and, indeed, the house is of vernacular design. Yet, its elements tend toward the elegance of Georgian style architecture, popular in its day, and which can be enjoyed today in profusion in the Colonial Williamsburg restoration in Virginia. Other elements tend toward the neoclassical school, which inspired most of the public structures in Washington, D.C.

The entrance facade of the Valentine–Varian House, which today faces Bainbridge Avenue, shows elements of all three styles. The material which forms the exterior walls is fieldstone, the rough uncut stone with their varied sizes and shapes that Isaac Valentine found on his land. They are held together with a mud-based mortar, which had been reinforced over the centuries with other materials, the latest being concrete. Despite the innumerable odd shapes and sizes of the stones, they are ingeniously placed to come to an aligned edge at each of the four corners of the building.

The doorway, in the center of the facade, is flanked by two evenly-spaced windows on either side. Above each window, on the second floor, is another window, slightly smaller in dimension, with a fifth window located directly above the doorway. Each has wooden shutters flanking it. The fenestration, with its pleasing symmetry and balance, may be found in the countless Georgian structures which survive from that era.

The portico of the doorway has a pediment, a feature of classical architecture. This classical element is emphasized by the fluted pilasters which flank the doorway itself.

The facade of the Valentine-Varian House may be compared and contrasted with that of the Van Cortlandt House in Van Cortlandt Park, which was built in 1748, only ten years before Isaac Valentine started construction. The Van Cortlandts had been a wealthy family for generations by the time their farmhouse was built, their fortune based upon their mercantile interests in New York City. Like the Valentine-Varian House, their farmhouse is made chiefly of fieldstone, and the fenestration of the entrance facades bear the same symmetry. Unlike the blacksmith's house, however, the Van Cortlandts lined their window settings with brick, and in each setting, just above the center of the window, is a carved face. Thus, the Valentine-Varian House's facade is simpler in design.

There are other significant differences between the two houses as well. The Valentine-Varian House is a simple rectangle in plan, while the Van Cortlandt House is L-shaped. The roof of the Valentine-Varian House is a simple pitched roof coming to a peak over the center of the rectangle, but the Van Cortlandt House has a mansard roof with three dormer windows on each side of the L to make its attic a habitable space. These elements give the Van Cortlandt House an elegant and interesting, but comparatively busy, facade, while the Valentine-Varian House's facade maintains a simple and quiet elegance, an aspect appealing to the modern eye.

The floor plan of the interior of the Valentine-Varian House is also simple and quite typical of its time and place. There is a central hallway leading directly to a stairwell and a rear door. On either side of the hallway are two rooms (four in total) with the two rooms in the front made appreciably larger than the two rooms in the rear. The hallway served an important function in the hot, humid summers common in the area. A Valentine, or, later, a Varian, merely had to open the doors at either end of the structure to have cooling breezes waft through the center of the house to provide relief in the days before electric fans and air conditioning were invented.

The typicality of the design can be demonstrated by a description of the tavern in the center of the town of Westchester, which was put up for sale in September, 1766, eight years after the Valentine-Varian House was built. William Betts, who owned the property, stated, "The House is two stories high, has four commodious rooms on each Floor, a Cellar under the whole, a good Garret and 9 Fire Places: The Entry is a spacious Passage thro' the Middle of the whole House, and contains a large Stair Case. . . . "[190] The description could be a double for that of the Valentine-Varian House, except that Isaac Valentine provided only eight fireplaces for his home, two each for each floor, the cellar, and the attic.

Because the house had been lived in continually from 1758 to 1960, and because of its modern function as a museum, details of the rooms inside have been changed over the years. Closets, cupboards, steam heat, and electric lights have been installed. Yet, many of the original architectural and construction elements have survived and still may be seen.

Many examples of these elements may be viewed in the room off the central hallway immediately to the left of the entrance. The wide, wooden boards, typical of the era, cover the floor, and those which are darker in color are the ones which Isaac Valentine laid himself. The lighter colored floorboards replaced those which had deteriorated over the years. Holding the original boards in place are many nails characterized by varied and odd-shaped heads, a sharp contrast to the perfectly round heads of modern nails. Undoubtedly, Isaac Valentine made these nails from his own blacksmith's forge.

In a recess in one corner of the room can be found a door made of similarly wide boards and hand-made iron hinges and nails. Originally, this door led to the passageway that had separated the house from the now-destroyed wing. Its construction suggests that the interior portion of the stone walls were lined with wide wooden boards, and such wide boards may be discovered in back of several of the closets added at a later date.

APPENDIX

Hand-hewn wooden elements may be found in other areas of the house as well. Most rooms still contain many of the original floorboards. A display in the room to the right of the entrance shows the hand-hewn chestnut laths held together with a mortar of mud, lime, and cow hair, and with Valentine's hand-forged nails. In the attic, the roof is supported by a remarkably large number of hand-hewn beams.

The last remaining original door in the Valentine-Varian House showing blacksmith Isaac Valentine's craftsmanship. Arthur Seifert, photographer. *The Bronx County Historical Society Collection.*

Only the larger rooms in the front of the building on either side of the central hallway have fireplaces. Because of this fact, it is probable that the winters were spent in the front rooms before the installation of central heating in the twentieth century.

West section of the attic of the Valentine-Varian House in 1971. The original hand-hewn beams placed by Isaac Valentine to support the roof still remain. They have been augmented by alternating them with newer, machine-sawed wood. *The Bronx County Historical Society Collection.*

The fireplace in the room to the left of the entrance is the only one in the house placed on a slightly raised platform. This, accompanied by the fact that the stones edge out from the floor of the fireplace to cover much of the platform, suggests that it was this fireplace which may have been used for

APPENDIX

cooking. The flames would heat the stones on the platform by convection, and, in turn, the stones would then be used to keep the already cooked food warm until it was ready to eat.

Looking at the windows from the interior of the building can give the observer an idea of the thickness of the fieldstone walls of the Valentine–Varian House. The walls are approximately two feet (60 centimeters) thick, with the windows placed closer to the outside portion of the wall than the inside. It is for that reason that the interior fenestration is splayed with the area on the inside portion of the wall far more open than the area on the outside portion. If the fenestration were straight, with the inside portion of the wall no wider than the outside portion, where the window is located, much of the sunlight coming through the window would hit that passageway without penetrating into the room itself, thus plunging the house into perpetual gloom. By splaying the fenestration, Isaac Valentine flooded his home with cheerful, airy sunlight, despite the thickness of the stone walls.

Architecturally, therefore, the Valentine–Varian House is a treasure. It is an excellent example of a typical farmhouse built in the area in the mid-eighteenth century. Moreover, the remarkable number of original architectural and construction elements which survive can inform observers not only about how such a house was built, but how the people who inhabited it really lived.

Overleaf: The restored Valentine-Varian House on its new site in 1975. *The Bronx County Historical Society Collection.*

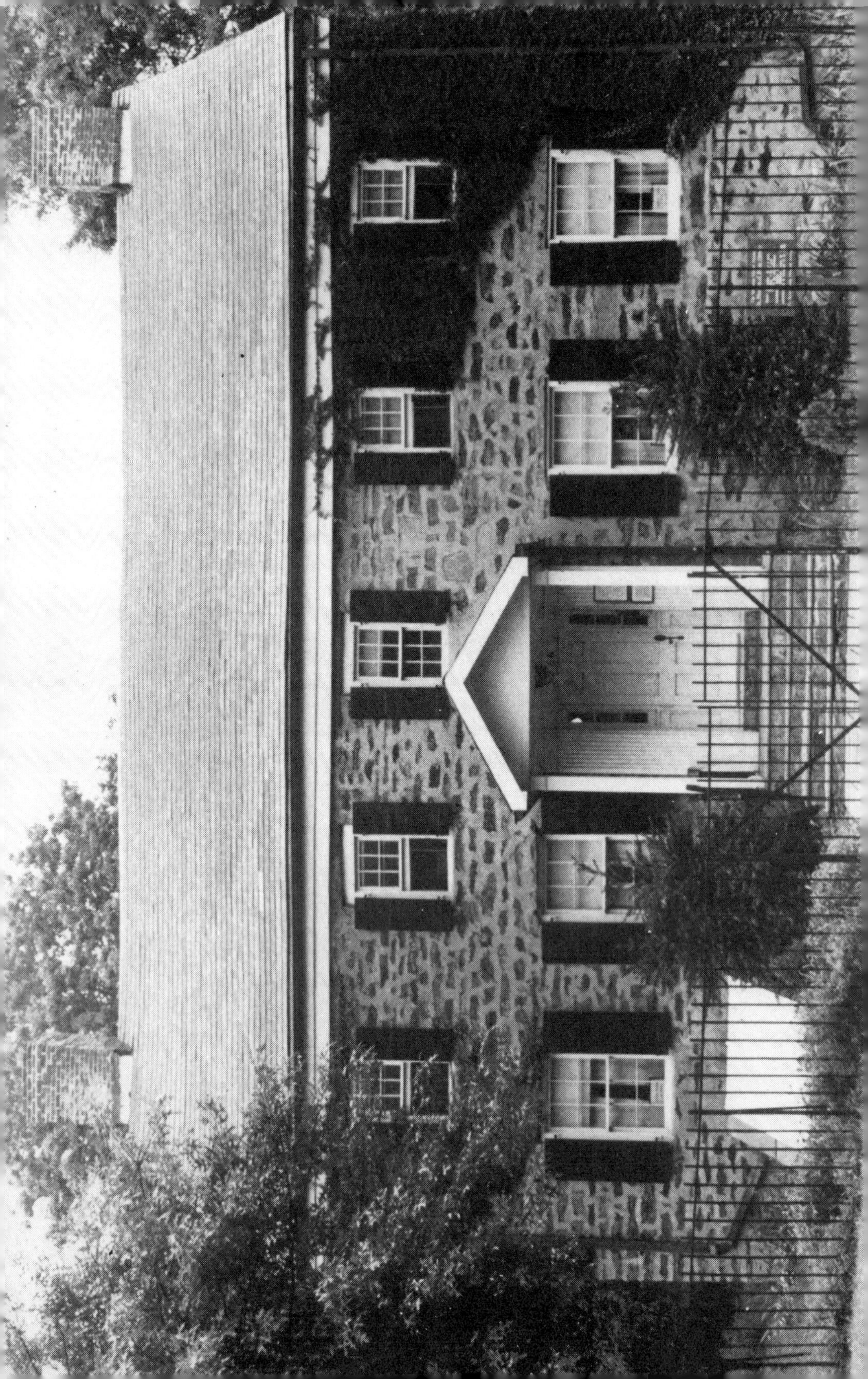

NOTES

CHAPTER TWO

1 *Ecclesiastical Records: State of New York*, ed. Hugh Hastings (Albany, J.B. Lyon Company, 1905), V, 3711-3712.

2 Stories about the old Boston Post Road may be found in Stephen Jenkins, *The Old Boston Post Road* (New York and London: G.P. Putnam's Sons, 1913); Sarah Comstock, *Old Roads from the Heart of New York: Journeys Today by Ways of Yesterday Within Thirty Miles Around the Battery* (New York and London: G.P. Putnam's Sons, 1915); Stewart H. Holbrook, *The Old Post Road* (New York, Toronto and London: McGraw-Hill Book Company, Inc., 1962); and Alice Fleming, *Highways Into History* (New York: St. Martin's Press, 1971).

3 Valentine's landed wealth is confirmed in E. Mary Becker, "The 801 Westchester County Freeholders of 1768," *The New-York Historical Society Quarterly*, XXXV (1951), 295-300, 312; and his family background is found in Grenville C. Mackenzie, "Early Records of the Valentine Families of Long Island and Westchester Counties" (Revised May, 1941), p. 9, typescript in the Local History and Genealogy Room, New York Public Library.

4 This controversy is documented in *The New-York Gazette: or the Weekly Post-Boy*, November 20, 1758; December 18, 1758; January 1, 1759; *The New-York Gazette; or the Weekly Post-Boy*, August 14, 1766.

5 *The New-York Journal, or General Advertiser*, March 5, 1767.

6 *The New-York Gazette; and the Weekly Mercury*, July 19, 1773.

7 *Ibid.*, March 23, 1772.

8. Montgomery's progress is found in *Ibid.*, August 2, 1773; October 4, 1773; *Rivington's New-York Gazetteer; or the Connecticut, Hudson's River, New-Jersey, and Quebec Weekly Advertiser*, October 14, 1773.

9 Records of Tetard's school are found in *The New-York Gazette; and the Weekly Mercury*, August 24, 1772; *The New-York Journal; or, the General Advertiser*, March 11, 1773.

10 *The New-York Journal; or, the General Advertiser*, June 25, 1772.

CHAPTER THREE

11 *Ibid.*, October 6, 1774; *Rivington's New-York Gazetteer; or the Connecticut, Hudson's River, New-Jersey, and Quebec Weekly Advertiser*, October 6, 1774.

12 *American Archives*, ed. Peter Force, 4th Ser., II, 1259; *Journals of the Continental Congress* (Washington: U.S. Government Printing Office, 1905), II, 59.

NOTES

13 *Public Papers of George Clinton, First Governor of New York, 1777–1795—1804-1804* (New York and Albany: Wynkoop Hallenbeck Crawford Company, 1899), I, 196.

14. *Rivington's New-York Gazetteer; or the Connecticut, Hudson's River, New-Jersey, and Quebec Weekly Advertiser,* June 29, 1775.

15. *Ibid.*

16. *American Archives,* 4th Ser., III, 150, 262, 466.

17 *Ibid.,* 4th Ser., III, 262.

18 *Ibid.,* 4th Ser., III, 465–466.

19 *Ibid.,* 4th Ser., III, 690–691, 879, 1130.

20 *Ibid.,* 4th Ser., III, 260–261, 890.

21 *Ibid.,* 4th Ser., IV, 1090.

22 The story of the spiked cannon can be followed in *Ibid.*, 4th Ser., IV, 1067–1069, 1072, 1083–1090, 1095, 1101–1102; V, 343–346; 5th Ser., I, 856–857; *The New-York Gazette: and the Weekly Mercury,* January 29, 1776; statement of Augustus Cregier, November 17, 1846, J.M. McDonald Papers, vol. 3, p. 375, Huguenot Historical Society, New Rochelle, N.Y.

23 *American Archives,* 4th Ser., V, 345–346; 5th Ser., II, 856.

24 Otto Hufeland, *Westchester County during the American Revolution: 1775-1783* (White Plains: Westchester County Historical Society, 1926), pp. 99–100.

25 The disposition of the cannon can be found in "Journal of Solomon Nash, a Soldier of the Revolution. 1776–1777.," *Crumbs for Antiquarians,* ed. Charles I. Bushnell (New York: Privately Printed, 1864), I, 19, 21; *American Archives,* 5th Ser., I, 1514.

26 The beginnings of the building of the forts can be found in *American Archives,* 4th Ser., VI, 992; *The New-York Gazette: and the Weekly Mercury,* June 24, 1776.

27 The beginning of military activity of the area are found in *American Archives,* 5th Ser., I, 20, 27–28, 225, 504–506, 790, 884–886, 915, 1030, 1143, 1494–1495, 1514; *Public Papers of George Clinton,* I, 298–299, 310; William Heath, *Memoirs of Major General William Heath,* ed. William Abbatt (New York: William Abbatt, 1901), p. 45; Orderly Books of Captain Bernardus Swartwout's Company of Lt. Col. Jacobus Swartwout's Regiment August 1776–February 1777, entry of August 23, 1776, New-York Historical Society; Orderly Book of Colonel Thomas Thomas, New York Militia August 17–October 5, 1776, entry of August 22, 1776, Library of Congress.

28 *American Archives,* 5th Ser., II, 856.

29 *Ibid.,* 5th Ser., I, 1560.

30 *Ibid.,* 5th Ser., I, 1563; *The Writings of George Washington,* ed. John C. Fitzpatrick (Washington: United States Government Printing Office, 1932), VI, 3.

31 These preparations are found in *American Archives,* 5th Ser., II, 855–856, 907–910; Heath, p. 59; Swartwout's Orderly Book, October 6, 1776, New-York Historical Society.

NOTES

32 *American Archives*, 5th Ser., II, 1035–1036, 1096–1097.

33 Heath, p. 64. Editor William Abbatt's note on the same page indicating that Heath's reference to "Valentine's" here refers to Valentine's Hill in Yonkers is obviously in error, since Heath identifies it as "the nearest to West Chester," and Isaac Valentine's house is nearer to Westchester than Valentine's Hill.

34 References to the home guard and the patrols are in Swartwout's Orderly Book, October 19, 1776, New-York Historical Society; U.S. Army Orderly Book of Col. M. Graham's Regiment October 12, 1776–December 20, 1776, entry of October 19, 1776, photostat, New York Public Library.

35 The evacuation story is in "Journal of Solomon Nash," *Crumbs for Antiquarians*, I, 38; *American Archives*, 5th Ser., II, 1164–1165; Heath, p. 65.

36 *Public Papers of George Clinton*, I, 390.

37 *American Archives*, 5th Ser., II, 1250.

38 *Ibid.*, 5th Ser., II, 1263–1264, 1294.

39 These incidents are described in fragments in various sources. These are: *Ibid.*, 5th Ser., II, 1294; III, 923–924, 1058; Captain Johann Ewald, *Diary of the American War: A Hessian Journal*, ed. and tr. Joseph P. Tustin (New Haven and London: Yale University Press, 1979), p. 13; "Journals of Captain John Montressor," *Collections of the New-York Historical Society for the Year 1881* (New York: New-York Historical Society, 1882), 121. Hereafter the books in the series called *Collections of the New-York Historical Society* will be cited as *Collections NYHS*.

40 Records of pillaging and warnings against them are in Swartwout's Orderly Book, August 18, September 8, September 29, 1776, New-York Historical Society; Thomas's Orderly Book, August 18, September 29, 1776, Library of Congress.

41 *American Archives*, 5th Ser., III, 245–246; *Writings of Washington*, VI, 222–223.

42 *American Archives*, 5th Ser., III, 924; "Journals of Lieut.-Col. Stephen Kemble," *Collections NYHS for the Year 1883* (New York: New-York Historical Society, 1884), p. 96.

43 These movements are chronicled in "Journals of Kemble," *Collections NYHS 1883*, p. 99; "Orders of Gen. Sir William Howe," *Collections NYHS 1883*, pp. 407–409; *American Archives*, 5th Ser. III, 924.

44 "Orders by Howe," *Collections NYHS 1883*, pp. 408, 411, 413–414; statement of Dennis Valentine, 1844, J.M. McDonald Papers, vol. 1, pp. 113–114, Huguenot Historical Society, New Rochelle, N.Y.

45 "Orders by Howe," *Collections NYHS 1883*, pp. 410, 412–413, 415.

46 *Ibid.*, p. 414.

47 *American Archives*, 5th Ser., III, 858. This is the same Robert Rogers who is the subject of Kenneth Roberts's novel, *Northwest Passage*, which was made into a motion picture and which inspired a television series bearing the same name.

NOTES

48 *American Archives*, 5th Ser., III, 1301; *Public Papers of George Clinton*, I, 485-487.

49 *American Archives*, 5th Ser., III, 1416, 1430.

50 *Ibid.*, 5th Ser., III, 1416.

CHAPTER FOUR

51 Heath, pp. 97-98; *Writings of Washington*, VI, 472-473, 497, 502.

52 Heath, pp. 99.

53 Details of the attempt on Fort Independence and the Valentine-Varian House's role in it are found in *Ibid.*, pp. 99-105; *The New-York Gazette: and the Weekly Mercury*, January 27, 1777; "Journals of Kemble," *Collections NYHS 1883*, pp. 108-109.

54 Heath, p. 106; *The New-York Gazette: and the Weekly Mercury*, February 17, 1777.

55 Examination and Deposition of Marcus Christian, August 19, 1783, Westchester County Court of Oyer and Terminer Papers, New York Public Library.

56 These moves are found in *The New-York Gazette; and the Weekly Mercury*, March 24, 1777; Hufeland, p. 196; Robert Bolton, *The History of the Several Towns, Manors, and Patents of the County of Westchester*, ed. C.W. Bolton (New York: Charles F. Roper, 1881), I, 253-254, 254n.b.

57 These two incidents are chronicled in *The New-York Gazette: and the Weekly Mercury*, June 16, 1777; July 7, 1777.

58 "Orders by Howe," *Collections NYHS*, 1883, p. 468.

59 *The New-York Gazette: and the Weekly Mercury*, August 11, 1777.

60 Quoted in Hufeland, pp. 238-239.

61 *Rivington's New-York Gazette: or the Connecticut, Hudson's River, New-Jersey, and Quebec Weekly Advertiser*, October 11, 1777; *The New-York Gazette: and the Weekly Mercury*, October 13, 1777.

62 The background of these incidents can be found in *Correspondence and Papers of Samuel Blachley Webb*, ed. Worthington Chauncy Ford (New York: Privately Printed, 1893) I, 236, 385-386; *Public Papers of George Clinton*, II, 512-513.

63 This engagement is chronicled in *Rivington's New-York Loyal Gazette*, November 29, 1777; December 6, 1777; *The New-York Gazette: and the Weekly Mercury*, December 1, 1777.

64 *The Royal Gazette*, December 20, 1777; *The New-York Gazette: and the Weekly Mercury*, December 22, 1777.

65 *Facsimiles of Manuscripts in European Archives Relating to America 1773-1783*, ed. B.F. Stevens (Wilmington, Del.: Melifont Press, Inc., 1970; reprint of 1888 ed.) XII, document number 1236.

NOTES

CHAPTER FIVE

66 The disposition of the troops and the sham battle are detailed in *The New-York Gazette: and the Weekly Mercury*, May 4, 1778; "Orders by Maj.-Gen. Daniel Jones," *Collections NYHS 1883*, p. 624; *Public Papers of George Clinton*, III, 588; *The Royal Gazette*, June 6, 1778; July 18, 1778; John Graves Simcoe, *A History of the Operations of a Partisan Corps, called the Queens Rangers* (New York: Bartlett and Welford, 1884), p. 74.

66 Simcoe, pp. 75-76, 78.

67 The battle with the Stockbridge Indians is told in fragments in *Ibid.*, pp. 83-86; *The Royal Gazette*, September 5, 1778; *The New-York Gazette: and the Weekly Mercury*, September 7, 1778; Ewald, pp. 144, 146-147; "A New York Diary of the Revolutionary War," ed. Carson I.A. Ritchie, *The New-York Historical Society Quarterly*, L (1966), 227.

69 Ewald, p. 152.

70 Fragments of information about winter preparations and the destruction of the houses are in *Ibid.*, pp. 153-156; *The New-York Gazette: and the Weekly Mercury*, November 16, 1778; *The Royal Gazette*, November 18, 1778; Simcoe, pp. 92-93; Hufeland, pp. 269-270; Ewald, p. 158; "Journal of Lieutenant John Charles Philip von Krafft, 1776-1784," *Collections NYHS for the Year 1882* (New York: New-York Historical Society, 1883), p. 68.

71 Bits of information about the illicit cattle trade and of Olmstead's observations can be found in *Public Papers of George Clinton*, IV, 361-362, 431-432; Ewald, pp. 156-157.

72 Details of these raids are in *The Royal Gazette*, March 3, 1779; *The New-York Gazette: and the Weekly Mercury*, March 8, 1779; "Diary," ed. Ritchie, *The New-York Historical Society Quarterly*, L (1966), 412-413; Hufeland, pp. 281-282.

73 "Diary," ed. Ritchie, *The New-York Historical Society Quarterly*, L (1966), 419; "Correspondence of James Pattison," *Collections NYHS for the Year 1875* (New York: New-York Historical Society, 1876), p. 73; *Public Papers of George Clinton*, IV, 857-858; Ewald, p. 160.

74 *The Royal Gazette*, June 14, 1783; *The New-York Gazette: and the Weekly Mercury*, June 16, 1783.

75 *The New-York Gazette: and the Weekly Mercury*, July 19, 1779.

76 The disposition of the troops can be found in Heath, p. 197; Ewald, p. 173; "Journals of Kemball," *Collections NYHS 1883*, p. 182.

77 Ewald, p. 173.

78 "Journal of von Krafft," *Collections NYHS 1882*, pp. 90, 92-96, 200; *Writings of Washington*, XVI, 77.

NOTES

79 Heath, p. 199.

80 Information about this engagement is found in *Ibid.*, p. 201; Ewald, pp. 178-181; *The Royal Gazette*, October 9, 1779; *The New-York Gazette: and the Weekly Mercury*, October 11, 1779.

81 Details of this raid are in Hufeland, pp. 310-312; *Public Papers of George Clinton*, V, 401n; *The McDonald Papers*, ed. William S. Hadaway (White Plains: Westchester County Historical Society, 1927), II, 20.

82 *McDonald Papers*, II, 24-25; Ewald, pp. 182-183.

83 *The New-York Gazette: and the Weekly Mercury*, December 20, 1779; *The Royal Gazette*, December 22, 1779.

84 *The Royal Gazette*, January 19, 1780; January 22, 1780; *The New-York Gazette: and the Weekly Mercury*, January 22, 1780; Heath, p. 210; *Public Papers of George Clinton*, V, 461-463; Hufeland, p. 323.

85 *The Royal Gazette*, March 11, 1780; *The New-York Gazette: and the Weekly Mercury*, March 13, 1780.

86 Quoted in Hufeland, p. 368; *A Revolutionary War Journal of Henry Dearborn: 1775-1783*, eds. Lloyd A. Brown and Howard H. Peckham (Chicago: The Caxton Club, 1939), p. 209.

87 *The Royal Gazette*, July 29, 1780.

88 *Writings of Washington*, XXI, 68-69, 139, 152, 160, 166, 172-173; Hufeland, pp. 374-376.

89 This account of the action of July 3, 1781, is pieced together from many fragments of information. They are found in: Orderly Book: Washington's Headquarters Orders June-October 2, 1781, entry of 3rd July 1781, New-York Historical Society; *The Royal Gazette*, July 14, 1781; *The New-York Gazette: and the Weekly Mercury*, July 16, 1781; Sir Henry Clinton, *The American Rebellion*, ed. William B. Willcox (New Haven: Yale University Press, 1954), p. 307; *A Fragment from the Diary of Maj. John Hutchinson Buell* (Brattleboro, Vt.: Hildreth and Fales, 1887), p. 7; "Journal of von Krafft," *Collections NYHS 1882*, p. 142; *Writings of Washington*, XXII, 296-299, 301-304, 308-310, 321, 326, 329-331; *The Diaries of George Washington*, ed. John C. Fitzpatrick (Boston and New York: Houghton Mifflin Company, 1925), II, 232-233; *Journal of Henry Dearborn*, p. 212; *Public Papers of George Clinton*, VII, xi n., 107-108n; "Clermont-Crevecoeur Journal," *The American Campaigns of Rochambeau's Army*, tr. and ed., Howard C. Rice, Jr., and Anne S.K. Brown (Princeton, N.J., and Providence, R.I.: Princeton University Press and Brown University Press, 1972), I, 32; "Berthier's Journal," *American Campaigns of Rochambeau's Army*, I, 248-249; *Memoirs of the Marshall Count de Rochambeau, Relative to the War of Independence of the United States*, ed. and tr. M.E.W. Wright (Paris: The French, English and American Libary, 1838), p. 55; *The Revolutionary War Journal of Baron Ludwig von Closen: 1780- 1783*, tr. and ed. Evelyn M. Acomb (Chapel Hill: The University of North Carolina Press, 1958), pp. 89-90; *Memoirs of the Duc de Lauzun*, tr. C.K. Scott Moncrieff (London: George Routledge and Sons, Ltd., 1928), p. 201; statement of

NOTES

Andrew Corsa, October 7, 1848, J.M. McDonald Papers, vol. 5, pp. 692–693, Huguenot Historical Society, New Rochelle, N.Y.

90 Information about the Grand Reconnaissance and its relation to the area of Valentine's farm is found in "Journal of von Krafft," *Collections NYHS 1882*. pp. 144–145; *Writings of Washington*, XXII, 371; *Diaries of Washington*, II, 241–242; *Public Papers of George Clinton*, VII, 110n; "Clermont-Crevecoeur Journal," *American Campaigns of Rochambeau's Army*, I, 36–39; *Journal of Baron Ludwig von Closen*, pp. 98–100; statements of Andrew Corsa, October 27, 1849 and October 19, 1850, J.M. McDonald Papers, vol. 6, p. 917, vol. 7, p. 1032, Huguenot Historical Society, New Rochelle, N.Y.

91 Heath, pp. 304–305.

92 The disposition of the troops and the state of the fort are found in Ewald, p. 348; Hufeland, pp. 429, 431.

93 *Writings of Washington*, XXVI, 268–269.

94 *Ibid.*, XXVI, 307, 334, 405; *Public Papers of George Clinton*, VIII, 176.

95 Complaints about these depredations are filed among the British Headquarters Papers in the Royal Institution, London, with photostat copies in the New York Public Library.

96 *Writings of Washington*, XXVI, 477; XXVII, 10, 26.

97 *Ibid.*, XXVII, 241, 243, 255; *Public Papers of George Clinton*, VIII, 285; *Rivington's New-York Gazette, and Universal Advertiser*, November 26, 1783; Hufeland, p. 439.

CHAPTER SIX

98 Concern over the Hessian fly is chronicled in *The New York Packet. and the American Advertiser*, August 26, 1784; *The Daily Advertiser: Political, Historical, and Commercial*, January 15, 1787; January 16, 1787; March 31, 1787; *The New-York Packet*, January 16, 1787; January 19, 1787; *The Independent Journal: or, the General Advertiser*, January 17, 1787.

99 *Loudon's New-York Packet*, November 11, 1784; *The New-York Packet*, October 10, 1785; April 6, 1786.

100 *Loudon's New-York Packet*, November 11, 1784; November 29, 1784; February 14, 1785; *The New-York Packet*, June 19, 1786.

101 *Loudon's New-York Packet*, November 11, 1784; November 29, 1784; March 21, 1785; *The New-York Packet*, June 19, 1786.

102 *The New York Packet. and the American Advertiser*, September 20, 1784.

103 *Loudon's New-York Packet*, April 18, 1785.

104 *The Daily Advertiser: Political, Historical, and Commercial*, June 17, 1786.

105 The transaction can be found in Westchester County Mortgages, Liber D, p. 37; Westchester County Deeds, Liber K., p. 125; the relationship

NOTES

between the two is confirmed in Mackenzie, "Valentine Families," p. 9, Local History and Genealogy Room, New York Public Library.

106 Westchester County Deeds, Liber K, p. 127.

107 The debt is found in Westchester County Mortgages, Liber C., p. 232; while the order for sale is in *The New-York Journal, and Weekly Register*, May 31, 1787.

108 *The New-York Packet*, May 1, 1786.

109 *The Independent Journal: or, the General Advertiser*, May 28, 1788.

110 Westchester County Deeds, Liber K, p. 141.

111 Westchester County Mortgages, Liber D, p. 291.

112 *The Daily Advertiser*, August 20, 1788; August 29, 1788.

113 *The New-York Packet*, July 24, 1786; September 14, 1786; June 29, 1787.

114 *The Daily Advertiser*, April 21, 1789.

115 *Diaries of Washington*, IV, 20–21.

116 *The Daily Advertiser*, June 4, 1790; January 17, 1792.

117 The number of slaves and members of the Valentine household can be found in *Heads of Families at the First Census of the United States taken in the Year 1790: New York* (Baltimore: Genealogical Publishing Co., Inc., 1971), p. 207; Valentine's economic standing is calculated from the list in *The Daily Advertiser*, January 15, 1791; and the family relations are in Mackenzie, "Valentine Families," p. 11, Local History and Genealogy Room, New York Public Library.

118 Westchester County Deeds, Liber K., pp. 128, 129.

119 *The Daily Advertiser*, June 4, 1790.

120 The two sales are advertised in *The New-York Journal and Weekly Register*, February 21, 1791; *The Daily Advertiser*, January 17, 1792.

121 The sale is recorded in Westchester County Deeds, Liber R, p. 315; that Valentine moved to White Plains can be found in statement of Andrew Corsa, September 24, 1847, J.M. McDonald Papers, vol. 4, p. 520, Huguenot Historical Society, New Rochelle, N.Y.

CHAPTER SEVEN

122 Samuel Briggs, *The Book of the Varian Family: With Some Speculation as to Their Origin, Etc.* (Cleveland: Theo. C. Schenck & Co., 1881), pp. 50–52.

123 "Federal Census, 1800: Westchester County, New York," *The New York Genealogical and Biographical Record*, LIX (1928), 35.

124 Westchester County Mortgages, Liber G, p. 445; Liber H, p. 101.

125 "Report by the Treasurer of the Trustees to the Annual Town Meeting on the fourth of April 1815," Town of Westchester, Records, Minutes of the Trustees 1 April, 1788–3 April, 1827, vol. 59, pp. 77–78, microfilm reel TWC 3, Paul Klapper Library, Queens College.

126 Westchester County Deeds, Liber P, p. 33; Liber Q, p. 50.

NOTES

127 Westchester County Mortgages, Liber T, p. 216.

128 Details of the Varian family's births, deaths, and marriages are in Briggs, pp. 50–54, 57.

129 Westchester County Deeds, Liber U, p. 161.

130 Briggs, pp. 50–51, 53; that Jane Varian was insane is stated in Westchester County Deeds, Liber V, p. 306.

131 Family matters are in Briggs, pp. 50–51; while details of the disposition of the farm can be followed in Westchester County Deeds, Liber V, p. 306; Liber X, p. 495; Liber Y, p. 173; Liber 28, p. 91; Westchester County Mortgages, Liber X, pp. 436, 437.

132 Westchester County Mortgages, Liber Z, pp. 244, 247.

133 Family matters are in Briggs, pp. 51, 55; the sale can be found in Westchester County Deeds, Liber 37, p. 265; and Westchester County Mortgages, Liber 33, p. 129; see also Randall Comfort, *et al.*, *History of Bronx Borough: City of New York* (New York: North Side News Press, 1906), p. 261.

134 Thomas F. Gordon, *Gazetteer of the State of New York* (Philadelphia: T.K. and P.G. Collins, 1836), p. 766.

135 Westchester County Mortgages, Liber 39, p. 222; Liber 55, p. 109.

136 *Ibid.*, Liber 272, pp. 1, 6, 11.

137 *Ibid.*, Liber 55, p. 109; Liber 284, p. 407.

138 *Ibid.*, Liber 397, pp. 470, 475.

139 *Ibid.*, Liber 33, pp. 121, 222; Liber 272, pp. 1, 6, 11; Liber 397, pp. 470, 475.

140 *Ibid.*, Liber 397, pp. 470, 475; Liber 493, p. 413.

141 Briggs, p. 51.

142 Westchester County Mortgages, Liber 37, p. 440; family relationships are in Briggs, p. 51.

143 Briggs, p. 57.

144 *Ibid.*, pp. 55–56.

145 *Ibid.*, pp. 69–70; Comfort, *et al.*, p. 261; James L. Wells, *et al.*, *The Bronx and Its People: A History* (New York: The Lewis Historical Publishing Co., Inc., 1927), IV, 128.

146 Westchester County Mortgages, Liber 272, p. 1.

147 Briggs, p. 55.

148 Comfort, *et al.*, p. 261; *Trow's New York City Directory* (New York: The Trow City Directory Company, 1885), XCIX, Varian, Jesse H.

149 Stephen Jenkins, *The Story of the Bronx* (New York and London: G.P. Putnam's Sons, 1912, p. 357.

150 Comfort, *et al.*, p. 261.

151 *Trow's New York City Directory* (New York: Trow Directory, Printing and Bookbinding Company, 1893), CVII, Varian, Jesse H.

152 *Ibid.*, CVX, Varian, Isaac; Varian, Jesse H.

153 New York County Mortgages, Section 12, Liber 12, p. 390.

154 New York County Deeds, Section 12, Liber 19, p. 412; New York County Mortgages, Section 12, Liber 21, p. 490; Liber 28, p. 47.

NOTES

155 New York County Deeds, Section 12, Liber 19, p. 408; New York County Mortgages, Section 12, Liber 12, p. 390; Liber 21, p. 490; Liber 28, p. 47.

156 New York County Deeds, Section 12, Liber 23, p. 62; New York County Mortgages, Section 12, Liber 29, p. 78.

157 "William C. Beller: In Memoriam," *The Bronx County Historical Society Journal*, XII (1975), 54; Esther Hoffman Beller to Gary Hermalyn, May 12, 1977, Correspondence Files, The Bronx County Historical Society.

158 Beller to Hermalyn, May 12, 1977, Correspondence Files, The Bronx County Historical Society; interview with Mrs. Esther Hoffman Beller, March 9, 1982.

159 "The Isaac Varian Homestead," Report Compiled May 4, 1934, by Thomas W. Hotchkiss for the historic American Buildings Survey, p. 4, typescript, Valentine-Varian House Papers, The Bronx County Historical Society.

160 *Ibid.*, p. 3.

161 *Ibid.* Seven of the blueprints may also be found in the Valentine-Varian House Papers, The Bronx County Historical Society.

162 "William C. Beller: In Memoriam," *The Bronx County Historical Society Journal*, XII (1975), 54; Beller to Hermalyn, May 12, 1977, Correspondence Files, The Bronx County Historical Society.

163 M.W. Del Gaudio, "Alteration to Dwelling Located at Bainbridge Ave. & Van Cortlandt Ave. E. Bronx, N.Y.," blueprints, July 26, 1936, Valentine-Varian House Papers, The Bronx County Historical Society.

164 Beller to Hermalyn, May 12, 1977, Correspondence Files, The Bronx County Historical Society; interview with Mrs. Beller, March 9, 1982.

165 New York Supreme Court, Appellate Division–First Department: Cole Export Import Co., Inc., Plaintiff-Appellant, against William C. Beller, Defendant-Respondent, *Papers on Appeal from Order*, Index No. 7421/1960, p. 52, hereafter referred to as *Papers on Appeal*. A copy is in the Valentine-Varian House Papers, The Bronx County Historical Society.

166 *Papers on Appeal*, pp. 18–28.

167 Bert Gumpert to Joseph Duffy, December 14, 1959, Correspondence Files, The Bronx County Historical Society.

168 *Papers on Appeal*, pp. 29–32.

169 Minutes of the Meeting of February 3, 1960, Minutes Files, The Bronx County Historical Society.

170 Minutes of the Meeting of March 2, 1960, Minutes Files, The Bronx County Historical Society; *Papers on Appeal*, pp. 46–47, 50, 53.

171 Minutes of the Meeting of April 6, 1960, Minutes Files, The Bronx County Historical Society.

172 Beller to Hermalyn, May 12, 1977, Correspondence Files, The Bronx County Historical Society.

173 *Papers on Appeal*, pp. 33–45.

174 *Ibid.*, pp. 45–48.

175 *Ibid.*, pp. 57–62.

NOTES

176 New York Supreme Court Appellate Division–First Department: Cole Export Import Co., Inc., Plaintiff-Appellant, against William C. Beller, Defendant-Respondent, *Appellant's Brief*, Valentine-Varian House Papers, The Bronx County Historical Society.

177 New York Supreme Court Appellate Division: First Department, Cole Export-Import Co., Inc., Plaintiff-Appellant, against William C. Beller, Defendant-Respondent, Agreement, November 16, 1960, Valentine-Varian House Papers, The Bronx County Historical Society.

178 Supreme Court of the State of New York: County of Bronx, Cole Export Import Co., Inc., Plaintiff, against William C. Beller, Defendant, Agreement, May 24, 1963, Valentine-Varian House Papers, The Bronx County Historical Society.

179 Beller to Hermalyn, May 12, 1977, Correspondence Files, The Bronx County Historical Society.

180 "Vandals Battering 1775 House Planned for Museum in Bronx," *New York Times* (August 22, 1963), p. 29, col. 6.

181 "Personality: Dr. Yesterday: Theodore Kazimiroff, D.D.S. is the county's official historian," *New York Journal American, Pictorial Living Special Section, The Bronx: Its People Its Progress Celebrating its 50th year as a county* (January 19, 1964), pp. Bx28–Bx29.

182 "Bronx of Yesteryear Is Being Preserved for Bronx of Tomorrow: City Clears Way to Move Crumbling Varian House," *New York Times* (November 7, 1964), p. 29, col. 6.

183 Bronx County Deeds, Section 12, Liber 2656, p. 154.

184 "Varian House, Built in 1770, Is Moved To New Bronx Site," *New York Times* (July 2, 1965), p. 60, col. 1; Minutes of the Meeting of July 6, 1965, Minutes Files, The Bronx County Historical Society.

185 Minutes of the Board of Trustees, June 21, 1966, Minutes Files, The Bronx County Historical Society.

186 Minutes of the Board of Trustees, November 15, 1966, Minutes Files, The Bronx County Historical Society.

187 "William C. Beller: In Memoriam," *The Bronx County Historical Society Journal*, XII (1975), p. 55.

188 Landmarks Preservation Commission, March 15, 1966, Number 1, LP-0119, Varian House, Valentine–Varian House Papers, The Bronx County Historical Society.

189 Minutes of the Board of Trustees, June 21, 1978, Minutes Files, The Bronx County Historical Society.

APPENDIX

190 *New York Gazette; or, the Weekly Post-Boy*, September 4, 1766.

BIBLIOGRAPHY

Unpublished Manuscripts and Documents

British Headquarters Papers. Photostat. New York Public Library.

Bronx County Deeds. Bronx Office, New York City Register.

Bronx County Mortgages. Bronx Office, New York City Register.

Correspondence Files. The Bronx County Historical Society.

Mackenzie, Grenville C. "The Early Records of the Valentine Families of Long Island and Westchester Counties." Revised: May, 1941. Typescript. Local Genealogy and History Room, New York Public Library.

McDonald, J.M. Papers. Huguenot Historical Society, New Rochelle, N.Y.

Minutes Files. The Bronx County Historical Society.

New York County Deeds. Bronx Office, New York City Register.

New York County Mortgages. Bronx Office, New York City Register.

Orderly Book of Colonel Thomas Thomas, New York Militia: August 17–October 5, 1776. Library of Congress.

Orderly Books of Captain Bernardus Swartwout's Company of Lt. Col. Jacobus Swartwout's Regiment: August, 1776–February, 1777. New-York Historical Society.

U.S. Army Orderly Book of Col. M. Graham's Regiment: October 12, 1776–December 20, 1776. Photostat. New York Public Libary.

Valentine–Varian House Papers. The Bronx County Historical Society.

Westchester County Court of Oyer and Terminer. Depositions. New York Public Library.

Westchester County Deeds. Bronx Office, New York City Register.

Westchester County Mortgages. Bronx Office. New York City Register.

Westchester, Town of. Records. Microfilm. Paul Klapper Library, Queens College.

Published Manuscripts

Buell, John Hutchinson. *A Fragment from the Diary of Maj. John Hutchinson Buell.* Brattleboro, Vt., 1887.

Bushnell, Charles I., ed. *Crumbs for Antiquarians.* New York, 1864.

Clinton, Sir Henry. *The American Rebellion.* Ed., William B. Willcox. New Haven, 1954.

Collections of the New-York Historical Society for the Year 1875. New York, 1876.

Collections of the New-York Historical Society for the Year 1881. New York, 1882.

Collections of the New-York Historical Society for the Year 1882. New York, 1883.

Collections of the New-York Historical Society for the Year 1883. New York, 1884.

Dearborn, Henry. *A Revolutionary War Journal of Henry Dearborn: 1775-1783.* Eds., Lloyd A. Brown and Howard H. Peckham. Chicago, 1939.

Ewald, Captain Johann. *Diary of the American War: A Hessian Journal.* Ed. and tr., Joseph P. Tustin. New Haven and London, 1979.

Heath, William. *Memoirs of Major General William Heath.* Ed., William Abbatt. New York, 1901.

Lauzun, Duc de. *Memoirs of the Duc de Lauzun.* Tr., C.K. Scott Montcrieff. London, 1928.

Rice, Howard C. and Anne S.K. Brown, tr. and ed. *The American Campaigns of Rochambeau's Army.* 2 vols. Princeton, N.J. and Providence, R.I., 1972.

Rochambeau, Comte de. *Memoirs of the Marshall Count de Rochambeau, Relative to the War of Independence of the United States.* Ed. and tr., M.E.W. Wright. Paris, 1838.

Simcoe, John Graves. *A History of the Operations of a Partisan Corps, called the Queens Rangers.* New York, 1884.

von Closen, Ludwig. *The Revolutionary War Journal of Baron Ludwig von Closen: 1780-1783.* Tr. and ed., Evelyn M. Acomb. Chapel Hill, N.C., 1958.

Washington, George. *The Diaries of George Washington.* 4 vols. Ed., John C. Fitzpatrick. Boston and New York, 1925.

───────────. *Writings of George Washington.* 39 vols. Ed., John C. Fitzpatrick. Washington, 1931–1944.

Webb, Samuel Blachley. *Correspondence and Papers of Samuel Blachley Webb.* 3 vols. Ed., Worthington Chauncey Ford. New York, 1893.

Published Documents

Clinton, George. *Public Papers of George Clinton, First Governor of New York 1777–1795—1801–1804.* 10 vols. New York and Albany, 1899–1914.

Force, Peter, ed. *American Archives.* 9 vols. Washington, 1837–1853.

Hastings, Hugh, ed. *Ecclesiastical Records: State of New York.* 5 vols. Albany, 1905.

Heads of Families at the First Census of the United States taken in the Year 1790: New York. Baltimore, 1971.

Journals of the Continental Congress. 34 vols. Washington, 1904–1946.

Stevens, B.F., ed. *Facsimile of Manuscripts in European Archives Relating to America 1773–1783.* 25 vols. Wilmington, Del., 1970.

Newspapers

The Daily Advertiser.
The Daily Advertiser: Political, Historical, and Commercial.
The Independent Journal: or, the General Advertiser.
Loudon's New-York Packet.
The New-York Gazette; and the Weekly Mercury.
The New-York Gazette: or the Weekly Post-Boy.
New York Journal-American.
The New-York Journal, or General Advertiser.
The New-York Packet.
The New-York Packet. and the American Advertiser.
New York Times.
Rivington's New-York Gazeteer; or the Connecticut, Hudson's River, New-Jersey, and Quebec Weekly Advertiser.

Rivington's New-York Gazette, and Universal Advertiser.
Rivington's New-York Loyal Gazette.
The Royal Gazette.

Interview

Beller, Esther Hoffman. Interview. March 2, 1982.

Books

Bolton, Robert. *The History of the Several Towns, Manors, and Patents of the County of Westchester.* 2 vols. Ed., C.W. Bolton. New York, 1881.

Briggs, Samuel. *The Book of the Varian Family: With Some Speculation as to Their Origin, Etc.* Cleveland, 1881.

Comfort, Randall, et al. *History of Bronx Borough: City of New York.* New York, 1906.

Comstock, Sarah. *Old Roads from the Heart of New York: Journeys Today by Ways of Yesterday Within Thirty Miles Around the Battery.* New York and London, 1915.

Fleming, Alice. *Highways Into History.* New York, 1971.

Gordon, Thomas F. *Gazeteer of the State of New York.* Philadelphia, 1836.

Hadaway, William S., ed. *The McDonald Papers.* 2 vols. White Plains, 1927.

Holbrook, Stewart H. *The Old Post Road.* New York, Toronto and London, 1962.

Hufeland, Otto. *Westchester County during the American Revolution: 1775–1783.* White Plains, 1926.

Jenkins, Stephen. *The Old Boston Post Road.* New York and London, 1913.

_____. *The Story of the Bronx from the Purchase Made by the Dutch from the Indians in 1639 to the Present Day.* New York, 1912.

Trow's New York City Directory. New York, 1885.
Trow's New York City Directory. New York, 1893.
Trow's New York City Directory. New York, 1895.

Wells, James L., et al. *The Bronx and Its People: A History.* 4 vols. New York, 1927, 1935.

Periodicals

Becker, E. Mary. "The 801 Westchester County Freeholders of 1768," *The New-York Historical Society Quarterly* XXV (1951), 283–315.

"Federal Census, 1800: Westchester County, New York," *The New York Genealogical and Biographical Record* LIX (1928), 33–41.

Ritchie, Carson I.A., ed. "A New York Diary of the Revolutionary War," *The New-York Historical Society Quarterly* L (1966), 401–445.

"William C. Beller: In Memoriam," *The Bronx County Historical Journal* XII (1975), 54–55.

INDEX

A

Acker, James, 77
Adams, John, 64
Albany, 75
Albany Post Road, 27, 71
Archer, Martha Varian, 78, 82
Armand, Charles, 47

B

Backus, Major, 19
Bainbridge Avenue, 1, 85, 87, 88, 92, 94, 100
Barclay, David, 16
Bathgate, James, 73, 80
Bearmore, Major Mansfield, 46, 47
Beller, William Charles, 88, 89, 90, 91, 92, 93, 94, 95, 99; photograph, 92
Beller, William Frank, 84–85, 86, 88, 99
Berrien, Nicholas, 12, 13, 41
Betts, William, 70
Betts, William, tavern owner, 102
Bickell, Alexander Wilhelm, 47
Bogert, Cornelius J., 67
Boston, 4, 9, 11, 12, 17, 37, 61
Boston Post Road, 4, 8, 9, 11, 14, 19, 24, 25, 27, 29, 32, 34, 36, 37, 38, 43, 46, 61, 64, 65, 73, 80; see also Van Cortlandt Avenue East
Boston Road, 74
Briggs, Elizabeth, 73
Briggs, Elizabeth Varian, 69, 71, 72, 73
Briggs, Isaac, 73
Briggs, Mary, 73
Briggs, Samuel, 71, 72
British Legion, 46
Bronx Community College, 46, 47
Bronx County Historical Society, The, 90, 91, 92, 95, 97, 99
Bronx River, 3, 4, 12, 13, 14, 17, 19, 30, 34, 38, 39, 42, 47, 52, 54, 56, 79, 80
Bronx, The, 1, 53, 82, 99
Brooklyn, 82
Brown, Jonathan and Nicholas, 9
Bruin, Frederick, 4
Bryant, Captain Lieutenant David, 28, 31
Burgoyne, General John, 35, 37, 38, 44

C

Canada, 35
Cannon, on Gun Hill, 13–18; in Fort Independence, 18, 22; ordered to fire on Valentine-Varian House, 28; fired at light horsemen, 29; fired from Fort Independence, 30; crossing Williams's Bridge, 30–31, 38; fired at Emmerich's Chasseurs, 38
Christian, Marcus, 32, 34
Clason Point, 26
Clinton, George, as General, 18, 20; as Governor, 56, 58, 60; portrait, 21
Clinton, General Sir Henry, 35, 37, 42, 45, 46
Carleton, Sir Guy, 56, 58
Civil War, 80
Cocks, John, 16
Cole, Alexander, 88; see also Cole brothers
Cole brothers, 89, 90, 91, 92, 93
Cole, Daniel, 88; see also Cole brothers
Colonial Williamsburg, 100
Comfort, Randall, 87
Concord, 11
Continental Army, 26, 36, 45, 52

INDEX

Continental Congress, 11, 12, 17
Corbie, John, 16
Cornwallis, Lieutenant General Earl, 25, 54, 62
Corsa, Andrew, 73
Corsa, Isaac, 48
Corsa, Isaac, purchaser of Varian farm, 73
Coutant, Gilbert, 69, 71, 72, 73, 74, 75, 77
Coutant, Mary Varian, 69, 71
"Cowboys," 37, 46, 47, 48, 49, 50, 51, 52, 53, 54, 56
Cregier, Augustus, 16

D

Daughters of the American Revolution, 88, 89, 90
Declaration of Independence, 17, 41
DeLancey, Colonel James, 37, 38, 46, 47, 48, 49, 50, 51, 52, 56, 59
DeLancey, Colonel Stephen, 35
DeLancey's Mills, 24, 30
Delavan, Captain Samuel, 34
Del Gaudio, M.W., 88
Dickin, William, 14, 15
Diemar, Captain Ernst Friedrich von, 46
Dobbs Ferry, 22
Dutchess County, 9, 18, 26
Dutch Reformed Church, 3, 4, 63, 66, 67, 68
Dwight, Timothy, 36, 49
Dyckman, Jacob, 7
Dyckman, Jacobus, 73

E

Eastchester, 32, 34, 42, 43, 45, 46, 47, 50, 52, 53, 73
Emmerich, Andreas, as Captain, 38, 39, 40; as Lieutenant Colonel, 41, 42, 43, 45, 51

Emmerich's Chasseurs, 38, 40, 42, 44, 45, 46
Emmons, Thomas, 62, 63, 66, 67, 68
Erie Canal, 75
Erskine, Quartermaster General Sir William, 25, 44
Ewald, Captain Johann, 46, 47

F

Farmer's Free Bridge, 7
Ferris, Ann, 76
Ferris, Caleb, 16
Ferris, David, 71
Ferris, Joshua, 16
Fordham, Manor of, 3, 12, 13, 41, 45, 47, 67, 70, 73
Fort Independence, 18, 19, 20, 22, 24, 25, 29, 30, 31, 32, 34, 35, 38, 40, 42, 46, 49, 51, 52, 53, 54
Fort Number Eight, 46, 50, 51, 54, 56
Fort Washington, 22, 24, 25
Fowler, Thomas, 32, 34
French army, 50, 51, 52, 53, 54
French Protestant Church, 9

G

Gambaro, James, 87
Gidney, Isaac, 14
Gill, Lieutenant Erasmus, 46, 47
Glean, Martha, 63
Graham, Colonel Morris, 20
Graham, Lieutenant Colonel Lewis, 15
Grand Concourse, 25
Grant, Major, 35
Grant, Major General James Lee, 24, 25
Great Britain, 11
Greenburgh, 77
Greenwich, Connecticut, see Horseneck, Connecticut

INDEX

Gumpert, Bert, 90
Gun Hill Road, 17

H

Hanson, Alfred E., 82, 84
Harlem Bridge, 74
Harlem Heights, 19
Harlem River, 3, 19
Harlem, town of, 58
Hartford, 9
Hatfield, Colonel, 48
Heath, Major General William, 18, 19, 20, 22, 23, 26, 27, 28, 29, 30, 31; portrait, 28
Hessian fly, 60, 64, 65, 66
Hessians, 22, 23, 24, 25, 26, 29, 30, 31, 32, 35, 38, 42, 43, 44, 45, 46, 47, 49, 51, 52, 53, 60
Historic American Buildings Survey, 87
Home Guard, 20
Honeywell, Captain Israel, 54, 56
Horseneck, Connecticut, 44, 46
Howe, General Sir William, 17, 19, 20, 24, 25, 35
Hudson River, 25, 27, 35, 37, 44, 50, 62, 63
Hufeland, Otto, 87
Hughes, James M., 62
Hull, Lieutenant Colonel William, 49, 50
Hunts Point, 47
Hurricane, 63, 64, 66
Hyatt, Caleb, 63

J

Jane Varian Trust, 74, 75, 76, 77, 78
Jenkins, Stephen, 87
Jerome Avenue, 4, 17, 86
Jerome Park Racetrack, 80, 82
Jerome Park Reservoir, 82

K

Kazimiroff, Theodore, 90, 91, 93, 94, 95, 99; photograph, 97
Kensico Dam, 80
Kestnbaum, Nathan, 90, 91
King's Bridge, 4, 7, 9, 11, 12, 13, 16, 17, 18, 19, 20, 22, 27, 31, 32, 35, 37, 38, 40, 41, 42, 43, 44, 45, 46, 47, 48, 49, 50, 51, 52, 53, 56, 58, 63, 65, 74; construction of fortifications near, 11, 12, 17, 18, 21; British repair of fortifications near, 24; British occupation of fortifications near, 25; Hessian occupation of area near, 26; British dismantling of fortifications near, 46; Washington crosses to Harlem, 58
Kingsbridge, village of, 80
Knyphausen, Lieutenant General Freiherr Wilhelm von, 22, 24, 25, 49

L

Lasher, Colonel John, 22
Lauzun, Duc de, 50, 51, 52, 53, 54
Lent, Benjamin, 73
Lexington, 11
Lexington Avenue subway, 86
Lincoln, Major General Benjamin, 50, 51
Livingston, Robert R., 9
Lockwood, Captain, 48
Long Island, 19, 53, 60
Loreto, Charles A., 91
Lott, Abraham B., 13
Lownsberry, William, 14, 15
Lyons, James J., 89

M

Mamaroneck, 14, 45, 46

INDEX

Manhattan Island, 4, 7, 19, 22, 44, 46, 50, 53, 54, 58, 62, 79, 80, 82, 85, 88
Mapes, Daniel, 77
Maps, 5, 8
Maryland dragoons, 46
Massachusetts, 11
McCartney, Cornelius, 16
McComb, Alexander, 71
Merchants Coffee House, 62
Mifflin, General Thomas, 17, 18
Mile Square, 22, 58
Mile Square Road, 27, 42, 50, 52
Militia, 12, 13, 15, 19, 20, 22, 26, 27, 30, 31, 41, 48
Mill on Westchester Creek, 70, 71
Montgomery, Richard, 9, 18, 41, 73; portrait, 10
Montressor, Captain John, 22
Morris, General Lewis, 41
Morris, Richard, 41, 47, 57, 58, 66; house, 47, 48; portrait, 57
Morrisania, 20, 34, 47, 48, 53, 54, 56
Mosholu Parkway, 4, 29, 77, 82, 89
Mosholu Parkway Realty Company, 84
Mount Vernon, 82
Mount Vernon Estates, Inc., 93

N

National Register of Historic Places, 97
Negro Fort, 24, 25, 29, 30, 31, 39, 40, 42, 51, 59
New England, 14, 27, 74
New Jersey, 25, 26, 27
New Rochelle, 14, 22, 27, 44, 46, 64, 69
New York and Harlem Railroad, 79
New York City, 1, 3, 4, 7, 9, 11, 12, 13, 14, 15, 16, 17, 25, 26, 27, 31, 32, 37, 42, 46, 48, 50, 53, 54, 56, 58, 60, 61, 63, 64, 67, 68, 69, 70, 71, 73, 74, 75, 77, 80, 88, 92, 99
New York City Landmarks Preservation Commission, 97
New York City Parks Department, 90, 91
New York Committee of Safety, 13, 14, 15, 16, 23
New York Post, 90
New York Provincial Congress, 11, 13, 16
New York Society for the Promotion of Useful Knowledge, 60
New York State Convention, 17, 18, 26
New York Times, 92
New York Volunteers, 35
Nicholas Brothers, 94
North Castle, 49

O

Oak Point, 47
Olmstead, Captain, 44
Orange County, 18
Ossining,
 see Sing Sing

P

Palmer, Benjamin, 7
Parsons, Brigadier General Samuel Holden, 53
Pawling, Colonel Levi, 20
Peekskill, 44
Pelham Bay Park, 20
Pell's Point, 20
Peyster, John de, 67
Philadelphia, 9, 11, 12, 35
Philipse, Frederick, 7
Pillaging, by Americans, 23, 24, 26, 48, 58; by Tories, 26, 43, 48, 49; by French, 54
Pine's Bridge, 50
Pintard, Major, 64

INDEX

Plunder,
see Pillaging
Prices, of farm goods, 60, 61, 64
Prueschenck, Lieutenant Colonel Ernst Carl von, 51, 52
Purdy, Joseph, 14
Putnam, Major General Israel, 38; portrait, 39

Q

Quebec, 18
Queen's American Rangers, 25, 26, 30, 32, 34, 38, 42, 46

R

Reservoir Oval, 81
Revere, Paul, 11, 12
Rhinebeck, 9
Richmond, Virginia, 61
Rochambeau, Comte de, 50, 53, 54, 62; portrait, 55
Rogers, Colonel Robert, 25, 30, 32, 34; portrait, 33
Rouaire, Marquis de la,
see Armand, Charles
Rye, town of, 43

S

St. George's Crescent, 25
St. Peter's Church, 3
Saratoga, 38, 44
Schmidt, Major General Martin Conrad, 25
Scott, Brigadier General John, 27
Signorelli, Anthony, 94
Simcoe, Lieutenant Colonel John Graves, 42, 43
Sing Sing, 51
Sixth Avenue subway, 88
"Skinners," 37, 48, 54
Slaves, 7, 35, 59, 66, 70, 74
Spuyten Duyvil Creek, 3, 4, 25, 73

Spuyten Duyvil Hill, 22, 62, 63;
see also Tippet's Neck
Stagecoach service, 9–10, 61
Stamford, 82
Stark, Brigadier General John, 49
Stockbridge Indians, 42
Stony Point, 44, 45
Stratford, Connecticut, 61

T

Tarrytown, 47, 48
Teller's Point, 44
Tetard, John Peter, 9, 18, 41, 42, 45, 52
Thatcher, Dr. James, 49
Third Avenue Bridge, 74
Third Avenue El, 86
Thomas, Thomas, as Colonel, 18, 19, 43; as Westchester County Sheriff, 66
Throg's Neck, 19, 20, 50, 71
Tippet, William, 63
Tippet's Neck, 63, 73;
see also Spuyten Duyvil Hill
Tories, 14, 25, 26, 32, 35, 37, 38, 42, 43, 44, 45, 46, 48, 49, 58, 59
Trefin, Charles
see Armand, Charles
Tryon, Major General William, 43, 44
Tuckahoe, 48
208th Street, 1, 92
206th Street, 88

U

Ulster County, 18
Union Dime Savings Bank, 82, 84
United States Customs House, 85
United States Department of the Interior, 87
Upper New York Bay, 17

INDEX

V

Valentine, Elizabeth, 66
Valentine farm, purchase by Isaac Valentine, 4; operation of, 7–8; cannon guard on, 14–15; American troops stationed on, 20; British troops stationed on, 24; British hay supply on, 25; Queen's American Rangers quartered on, 25, 26; Hessian troops flee from, 27; troops behind stone wall on, 30; Tory and Hessian troops encamped on, 44; hay gathered on, 45; Jäger picket on, 47; Charles Armand's troops on, 47; subject to plunder, 48; DeLancey's troops occupy, 51; DeLauzun's troops on, 52, 53; French troops on, 54; effect of war on, 59; barn on, 64, 66, 67; sale of, 67–68
Valentine, Isaac, 4, 6, 7, 8, 9, 10, 11, 12, 13, 14, 15, 16, 17, 18, 19, 20, 22, 23, 25, 29, 32, 34, 35, 36, 37, 40, 41, 45, 54, 58, 59, 60, 61, 62, 63, 64, 66, 67, 68, 70, 71, 74, 99, 100, 102
Valentine, Isaac Jr., 12, 13, 14, 15, 62, 70
Valentine, John, 66
Valentine, John Jr., 70
Valentine, Peter, 14, 62, 66
Valentine's woods, 20, 51, 52
Valentine-Varian House, architecture of, 1, 6, 100–105; construction of, 6; robbery in, 9; Revere passes, 11, 12; Washington passes, 12, 65; cannon near, 13–18; serves as tavern, 16, 18; American troops at, 20; British troops at, 24; Hessian troops occupy, 26; battles involving, 27–29; 30–31, 34, 38, 38–40, 50–53; American troops occupy, 29; Robert Rogers in, 32; as jail, 34; proclamation posted on, 43; escaped demolition, 43; Captain Olmstead in, 44; Rochambeau in, 54; sold to Isaac Varian, 73, 74; sold to Michael Varian, 75, 76; known as Varian Homestead, 79; in New York City, 80; maintained by Jesse Huestis Varian, 81; possessed by Isaac Varian, 82; sold to Alfred E. Hanson, 82, 84; bought by William Frank Beller, 84; tenants in, 85, 88; renovation of, 85–86, 88; destruction of west wing, 86; receives attention of historians and architects, 87; first called, 87; inherited by William Charles Beller, 88; garage built, 88; second wing added, 88; land sold to Cole brothers, 89, 93; tenants leave, 91; court case involving, 91–92; vandalized, 93; removal to new site, 93–94; restoration of, 95; donated to Bronx County Historical Society, 95; opened as museum, 95, 96; declared historic landmark, 97; photographs, 81, 83, 85, 86, 87, 89, 95, 96, 98, 99, 103, 104, 106
Van Cortlandt, Augustus, 62, 66, 67, 70
Van Cortlandt Avenue East, 1, 4, 25, 92, 94
Van Cortlandt, Frederick, 63, 66
Van Cortlandt House, 24, 51, 101
Van Cortlandt Park, 101; lake in, 62
Van Cortlandt Park East, 27
Van Cortlandt family, 6
Van Cortlandt's mill pond, 62
Van Zandt, Peter P., 67
Varian, Alfred, 77
Varian, Alletta Harsen, 69, 71
Varian, Dorcas, 72
Varian, Catherine Washington, 69

INDEX

Varian farm, sold in 1820, 73–74; reduction in size, 74; sold in 1829, 75, 76; mortgages on, 76–77; in town of West Farms, 80; in New York City, 80; operated by Jesse Huestis Varian, 80; part taken for reservoir, 80–81; used for milk production, 82; sold in 1905, 82, 84
Varian, George Washington, 69
Varian, Gilbert Coutant, 72
Varian, Hannah, 72
Varian, Hannah Leggett, 72
Varian, Hannah Van Den Berg, 69
Varian Homestead
see Valentine-Varian House
Varian, Isaac, 68, 69, 70, 71, 72, 73, 74, 75, 80
Varian, Isaac Jr., 69, 71, 72, 73, 78
Varian, Isaac Leggett, 71, 78; photograph, 79
Varian, Isaac, son of Michael Varian, 78, 82
Varian, Jacob Harsen, 69, 72, 73
Varian, James, cousin, 73
Varian, James, son of Isaac, 72, 78
Varian, Jane, 72, 76, 77
Varian, Jane Betts, 72, 73, 74, 77
Varian, Jane, daughter of Michael Varian, 78
Varian, Jesse Huestis, 78, 80, 81, 82; photograph, 81
Varian, Lorinda Conklin, 81; photograph, 81
Varian, Martha Huestis, 75, 80
Varian, Michael, 72, 75, 76, 77, 78, 80, 81, 82, 99; photograph, 81
Varian, Michael, son of Michael Varian, 78
Varian, Richard, 69, 72, 74, 75, 77
Varian, Tamar Leggett, 69
Vault Hill, 51, 52
Vermillye, John, 4, 7, 9
Verplanck's Point, 44
Virginia, 54, 100

W

Ward, Aaron, 75, 76
Washington, George, 12, 17, 19, 20, 23, 25, 27, 50, 51, 52, 53, 54, 56, 58, 62, 65, 66
Waterbury, Brigadier General David, 53
Wayne, General Anthony, 45
Webster Avenue, 86
Westchester County, 3, 6, 7, 9, 12, 13, 15, 18, 23, 26, 35, 37, 38, 41, 44, 50, 53, 54, 56, 57, 60, 69, 75, 80
Westchester Creek, 70
Westchester Square, 12, 20
Westchester, town of, 3, 11, 12, 20, 26, 41, 45, 58, 59, 63, 66, 68, 70, 71, 73, 80, 102
West Farms, 12, 13, 24, 35, 36, 38, 48, 49, 50, 53, 69, 72
West Farms, town of, 80
Wheat, 59, 60, 64, 65, 66, 75, 76
White Plains, 21, 22, 27, 35, 37, 68, 77
Willett's Point, 26
Williamsbridge Oval Park, 1, 88, 94
Williamsbridge Reservoir, 80, 81, 88
Williamsbridge, village of, 80
Williams House, 24, 25, 30
Williams, John, 14, 16, 24
Williams's Bridge, 14, 15, 19, 27, 29, 30, 34, 38, 40, 42, 44, 46, 47, 48, 49, 50, 51, 52, 53, 54, 56, 80; redoubt near, 19, 20, 24, 25, 30, 34, 42, 59
Williams's farm, 14, 16
Woodlawn Cemetery, 19, 27, 80
Woodlawn Road, 85

Wooster, Brigadier General David, 27, 29
Wurmb, Colonel Ludwig Johann Adolph von, 47, 52

Y

Yale College, 36
Yonkers, 4, 22, 42, 43, 44, 45, 51, 53, 58, 62, 63, 67, 68, 70, 71, 72, 73, 94
Yonkers Savings Bank, 76, 77
Yorktown, 54, 62

THE BRONX COUNTY HISTORICAL SOCIETY

The Bronx County Historical Society was founded in 1955 for the purpose of collecting and preserving manuscripts, books, and historical objects concerned with the history, heritage, and growth of the Bronx, and to promote knowledge, interest, and research in these fields.

Administrators of
THE VALENTINE-VARIAN HOUSE
c. 1758
which houses
THE MUSEUM OF BRONX HISTORY
3266 Bainbridge Avenue at East 208th Street
and
EDGAR ALLAN POE COTTAGE
c. 1812
Poe Park, Grand Concourse at East Kingsbridge Road

The Bronx County Historical Society, with a broad memberhip base, maintains The Bronx Research Library and Archives; conducts historical tours and educational programs.

Producers of the "OUT OF THE PAST" radio show and publishers of a varied series of books, journals, and newsletters including
"THE BEAUTIFUL BRONX"
and
"THE BRONX COUNTY HISTORICAL SOCIETY JOURNAL"

Poe Cottage

For additional information, please write or phone:
THE BRONX COUNTY HISTORICAL SOCIETY
Research Library and Offices
**3309 Bainbridge Avenue, Bronx, New York 10407
(212) 881-8900**

VALENTINE-VARIAN HOUSE

c. 1758

MUSEUM OF BRONX HISTORY
THE BRONX HERITAGE CENTER

The Valentine-Varian House, owned and administered by The Bronx County Historical Society, was donated by Mr. William C. Beller.

Open Saturday 10:00 A.M.–4:00 P.M., Sunday 1:00 P.M.–5:00 P.M.
Guided Tours by appointment during week.

3266 Bainbridge Avenue at East 208th Street
Telephone: (212) 881-8900